Going Global on a Dime

*The Entrepreneur's Handbook
to Tapping the Global Marketplace*

Lauri E. Elliott

Published by Conceptualee, Inc.

Published by Conceptualee, Inc.:

301 McCullough Drive, 4th Floor
Charlotte, North Carolina 28262
United States

ISBN-13 9780983301561 Paperback
ISBN-13 9780983301578 Electronic Book
LCCN 2011914089
10312011

Chapter Contributors: Shelvin Longmire, William Northcote, and Joseph Price

Compilation Assistance by Christopher Wallace
Book Cover Design by Vin Furlong
Cover Background by Nimalan Tharmalingam
Globe on Front Cover by Jan K.

Business & Economics / International / General

Don't wait for extraordinary opportunities. Seize common occasions and make them great. Weak men wait for opportunities; strong men make them.

(Orison Swett Marden)

Other titles and content on insights, resources, and strategy for global business and investment can be explored at:

http://www.globalbizconcierge.com

http://www.goingglobalonadime.com

http://www.afribiz.info

Table of Contents

Preface
Lauri Elliott

The idea for *Going Global on a Dime* came after living and doing business in Africa (a region considered one of the most difficult to do business) successfully as an entrepreneur. When I returned to the U.S. and shared my experiences, one of the main messages I kept hearing from others was that they weren't empowered to do business globally. The reasons ranged from capacity to finances to connections.

While these issues are valid, I discovered that getting what I didn't have was not the answer, but using and leveraging what I did have made all the difference. Today, it's not what you own or have control over that determines whether you have the capacity to succeed globally, it's also what you can tap into – other people's expertise, resources, and connections.

What I focus on in this book is demonstrating pathways that many entrepreneurs can follow to enter and be successful in the global marketplace. There is no formula for success. It will hinge on your ability to discover and implement a unique pathway, shaped by the strengths you are able to leverage.

The name for the book comes from the entire approach to going global that my strategic partners and I have learned over the years. If you shape your global opportunity correctly, you will find that you spend 10% of what is normally spent to do so and you can leap at least ten steps forward for every one step you take in this new era of global entrepreneurs.

The *Going Global on a Dime* approach has many elements that you can employ to shape and structure a strategy for going global. This book focuses on providing a framework to go global in 12 to 18 months. It won't answer every question, but it will give you a clear framework to use as you find your own unique path for global success.

While I would be gratified if everyone read this book, it is not for the faint of heart. It can only help you if you can tap into the power of being an entrepreneur.

I look forward to sharing the going global journey with you.

Foreword

Shelvin Longmire

Chairman, Center for Global Entrepreneurship and Enterprise Management

"The emerging movements towards economic self-reliance will not be led by political action but by digital technology and creative entrepreneurship." Ron Watkins

Small businesses and entrepreneurs have a well-earned tradition and established track record for being major change agents in economies around the world: creating millions of new jobs; spearheading innovative and cutting-edge technologies; developing new and futuristic, first-to-market opportunities; and advancing the next generation of new business models and market strategies. Another advantage is that small businesses and entrepreneurs are normally less bureaucratic and depend more on personal interactions. Many small businesses continue to consider themselves to be social entrepreneurs - a characteristic that will serve them well in many emerging markets where some business cultures might be more focused on personal relationships than more formal business structures and protocols.

There is no doubt that enterprising entrepreneurial industries will continue to lead the way for prosperity and sustainable economic growth in this global economy.

The nimble and flexible nature of small businesses, coupled with the rapid advances in technology - instant global communications, faster modes of transportation, secure electronic trading platforms, etc. - has positioned small businesses to be the dominant global players in the 21st century. However, even with all of these fascinating push-button technical capabilities, it would be a serious mistake to overlook the consistent need for the necessary managerial expertise, the crucial cultural knowledge, and the critical social skills that are essential to our success in our chosen markets and ventures - machines don't do business, people do.

This era of the global entrepreneur excites me. So, when my good friend and colleague, Lauri Elliott, approached me about writing a foreword to her book I was extremely pleased to be able to make a small contribution to this very timely and worthy initiative. As an international trade consultant and strategic advisor on global business, I can sincerely appreciate the value of Lauri's hard work and dedication to this endeavor. Over the past decade or so, she has proven to be one of the most visionary evangelists and promoters of the entrepreneurial spirit; a strong advocate for free and fair trade; and a leading voice for leveraging innovative enterprises as a catalyst for creating prosperity and sustainable economies and communities across the globe.

For small and medium sized business owners and entrepreneurs that are exploring the possibilities of, or planning on, going global and for the many novices out there that are just curious to know what all of this international trade talk and "globalization" media hoopla is really all about, this book provides an excellent framework for often overlooked informal and social processes associated with going global rather than the technical pieces found elsewhere.

Although primarily written for new to market small businesses and entrepreneurs, seasoned global business practitioners will find that this book provides a refreshing summary, and some unique perspectives, on navigating the opportunities, challenges, and nuances of doing business in today's highly complex and competitive international business environment. Lauri delves into the mindset and strategies that should be considered and leveraged to successfully engage in the diverse political, cultural, economic, and social environments of the global markets.

Lauri goes beyond the "how to" basics of international trade. She selflessly shares her hard earned hands-on knowledge, her intellectual capital, and her professional insights on several important issues that are normally not addressed by other authors, such as the cultural and environmental aspects that should be considered or assessed for doing business in highly competitive international markets. In addition, to enhance the potential for sustainable and profitable overseas ventures, she takes it to the next level by concisely outlining some of the business models, enterprise strategies, resources, and leverage points for successfully accessing opportunities and performing in these markets.

Needless to say, long ago Lauri saw the handwriting on the wall while most small businesses and entrepreneurs were still convinced that they more or less had an exclusive on their local or regional markets. She was very much aware that those "local" markets were increasingly challenged by intense global competition from newly emerging markets for goods, services, customers, and brand recognition. Under these circumstances, this book is a very timely and well overdue resource for all of us that are convinced that global entrepreneurship is truly "the next big thing." The phrase, "think locally and act globally," has never been more relevant to the small business community.

Most of us have heard that business is a form of economic warfare, and ready or not the intensity and increasingly competitive nature of the global economy has come to bear on each and every one of us in one fashion or another. It might be way too late now for basic combat training, but Lauri has graciously armed us with the commander's field manual with practical guidelines that we can immediately put to use to facilitate our presence and enhance our performance in the global marketplace. This is her version of "The Art of War."

1

Introduction

Shelvin Longmire

Whether you're interested or not, you are part of the global economy. When you go to a Wal-Mart, or your local retail outlet, the goods you purchase are made elsewhere. We are all a part of the big picture called the global economy. Once you absorb this as part of your mindset, the idea of doing global business is not such a foreign concept.

Large firms and multinational corporations are thriving in the global economy. In regions like Africa and Asia, firms are experiencing returns on investment exceeding 30%. But the global marketplace is not just for the big boys, it's for people like you and me – entrepreneurs and small business owners.

In fact, there are tremendous opportunities for entrepreneurs and SMEs in emerging market countries waiting for someone like you to take advantage of them. Instead of finding too few opportunities, people get overwhelmed with the sheer number of them.

There are so many opportunities because these markets are growing. While Western developed nations will experience growth less than 3% annually for the next several years, countries like China, India, Ethiopia, and Ghana will grow at more than 7% per year. Ghana's growth is projected to be close to 20% between 2011 and 2012, according to the World Bank.

They are expanding, and they are in need of just about everything. They are open to everyone, but they require strong people with entrepreneurial spirits, as well as those who will venture out – pioneers, adventurers, and explorers. Or at least people, who will work with people and organizations with these characteristics.

Why does going global require these characteristics? Any business presents challenges, but global business brings a whole new set of issues that you have to handle well to be successful.

Challenges of Going Global

The first type of challenge is market entry issues, such as time and distance. Time differences and travel expenses can be a hindrance, but advances in technology today are shortening these gaps.

You also need to consider the suitability, or adaptability, of your product in the foreign market into which you are introducing it. Just because a good or service sells well in your country does not guarantee that it will find success in foreign markets.

Another consideration is will the good or service be offensive to a foreign culture (e.g., in the Middle East which has strict cultural norms)? Also, how does the product's name translate literally into the local language? It is not uncommon to change the name of products to appeal to foreign, or global, markets.

The next market entry issue is lack of adequate infrastructure (e.g., roads, electricity, telecommunications). This can impact another market entry issue, which is getting your product to the market. In other words, there can be challenges with transportation, logistics, and supply chains.

The second challenge type is environmental factors – climate, geography, and ecosystem. If you are trying to sell frozen food products in a desert country where freezers are a luxury, then you may want to rethink your game plan. If you are planning on setting up a manufacturing operation in a rural area, you will need to assess the infrastructure and roadways - they will be key to your operation. Many rural areas may not have roads that will support heavy traffic from heavy machinery, though sometimes nearby rivers can be used for efficient transportation.

The third type of challenge relates to business culture, customs, and protocol. It is not uncommon that business practices are informal and lack standard procedures, which can make it very difficult to navigate business in the foreign market. Some emerging markets, as far as their business practices go, are probably at the same place Western markets were over 75 years ago. Goods are often sold in open markets in the streets of even the largest cities in developing countries.

Bureaucratic institutions, inadequate regulatory environments, and political influence over commercial transactions are also issues. But, corruption seems to be the most talked about obstacle, and in some developing nations, is very rampant. Often, people and institutions in developing countries have different perceptions on what defines bribery and corruption. This is something of which you need to be cognizant.

If you are from a Western developed nation and operate in another country, you can find yourself in trouble over certain business practices. These business practices may not be illegal in your host country, but are in your home country. If you are a U.S. citizen, there are very strong laws that govern being involved in bribery and corruption overseas. For example, if you have to pay somebody on the side to get a contract or to get your product cleared through the port, these practices are considered to be unacceptable under U.S. law.

Overcoming the Challenges

So, if there are so many challenges, how can a small business or entrepreneur like you make it? First, do your research. Before doing business anywhere, whether abroad or domestically, it is important to know as much as you can about the market that you are entering. This is even more pertinent when you are doing business in an environment with which you are not familiar.

Before you even travel to the emerging country in which you plan to invest, it is important to do your homework. Fortunately, if your home country is a Western industrialized nation, you will typically find general market research and information made available through your government. In the U.S., information is available on almost every country in the world. (See list of resources in Appendix A.)

Find out what the political environment is. Is there political stability there or civil unrest? Is the leader of the country pro or anti-business? Is there a pro or anti sentiment amongst the population concerning your home country? How prevalent is crime? Will you need to hire private security?

You will also need to know how to deal with local bureaucratic regulations, starting with whether or not you can even do business there. You will also need to look into import, export, and business licenses. It will also be important to get familiar with their regulatory standards. This can all seem a little overwhelming, that is why it's a good idea to take care of as much of the paperwork as you can at home, that way you can hit the ground running once you travel to your new place of business.

When it comes to your interactions with the local government (they may seem unorganized and informal), keep in mind that they do have a system. Be persistent when you have to, but be careful not to be rude.

Another step to set yourself on a course for positive engagement is to learn about the culture and language. Even if you only learn the basics of the language, enough to get around town, it will show the locals that you are willing to learn and are open to things that are important to them. Even if you do not plan on visiting immediately, demonstrating a desire to learn more about the people and country you want to enter can go a long way once you get there.

At this stage, you probably don't see a clear path of how you can go global. You are feeling what many of us who have done it felt, and still feel at times. There is no formula for being successful in going global, but there are strategies and tactics you can learn that will carry you a long way. And for me, the key strategic advantage you can create for yourself is to form the right partnerships.

As a small business, you should partner with a company, either foreign or domestic, that already has established itself to some degree in the market you are looking to enter. While you will build partnerships elsewhere to take advantage of a particular market, you must have local partners. You have to have people that understand the politics, culture, language, and nuances of doing business on the ground in your host country. If you are visiting the country, it is important to have a close partner or someone that you trust as an interpreter when you are talking business.

We also need to keep the proper perspective on forming partnerships. Western businesses, particularly those from the U.S., expect things to be done within a certain time frame and done a certain way. In informal markets, time issues require a lot of patience. You may end up taking several detours before you are able to get some things done. Whether or not you get something done generally depends on the relationships you have built with the people with which you are dealing. Building a strong relationship with someone does not happen overnight. It will take time to develop relationships, time to manage them, and time to get the results that you want from them. Once your relationships strengthen, however, you will have extremely valuable allies.

Once you have a firm grasp on the fact that you will face challenges and that the cornerstone for your going global efforts needs to be partnerships, you will find there are many paths to help you take advantage of opportunities as you will have many more options, capabilities, and channels through those partners.

You can now look at what other strategies and tactics will help you go global. My first step is to look at what strengths, tangible or intangible, I possess that will carry me forward. They can be as concrete as cash or as esoteric as, say for example, the image of American products abroad. In this example, in pro-American markets where the image of American products is reliability and quality, you have an edge. However, you need to understand that it's not typically a single advantage that makes you successful; it's how you combine your strengths that can set you apart.

Another way to improve your efforts in going global is to focus on industry opportunities and strategies. Transferring technology to foreign markets, as long as it meets certain requirements dictated by individual countries, is a great way to do business in other countries. If you have new and innovative services or other products you think are marketable overseas, then do it!

You can also look at franchising opportunities. If you already have a business that would make a good franchise, you can contact organizations, e.g. the International Franchise Association[1] in the United States, that help franchises go global. The other route is to find franchises that are looking to enter global markets and take their franchise business model to another country.

Also, look at the agreements your country has with other countries that make unique importing, exporting, and global business opportunities and platforms. This path may reduce the challenge of getting your goods and services into another country.

There are also market entry portals that serve as "open doors" into other markets. One great option you have is commercial subcontracting. This is where you identify another company from your home country that is doing business in a specific industry and country and looking for partners or subcontractors. This happens a lot, especially in industries like oil and mining.

Other market entry portals include international development, governmental, and non-governmental institutions, such as the World Bank and regional development banks. If you are a U.S. company, the U.S. Agency for International Development (USAID)[2], United Nations (UN)[3], U.S. Trade and Development Agency (USTDA)[4], and the Millennium Challenge Corporation (MCC)[5] are great places to inquire about possible contracting and supplying opportunities overseas. In other highly developed nations like the U.K., you will find similar organizations.

---

[1] http://www.franchise.org
[2] http://www.usaid.gov
[3] http//www.un.org
[4] http://www.ustda.gov
[5] http://www.mcc.gov

You can also look to private sector channels like chambers of commerce and business councils. You can contact chambers from your home country that have branches or affiliates in foreign countries. For example, the U.S. Chamber of Commerce[6] has affiliate chambers in every region of the world.

Also, as eager as you may be to explore foreign markets, there are others who want to tap Western markets like the U.S. You can take advantage of this by forming a two-way trade partnership. This way you can partner with a business savvy person in a market of your choosing. While you help them get established here in the U.S., they can help you get established in their country. You can make contact with firms like this through embassies[7] and chambers of commerce.

As a final note, something also must be said about how you should do business in another country, particularly developing countries. While you want to make a profit, you must also consider people and the planet, this is called the triple bottom line. A lot of people in emerging markets have been treated poorly and taken advantage of in the past, exploited by foreigners who extract resources from their land and then leave. Developing nations don't want you to come to their country and just sell a product or service, they are looking for mutual partnerships in which you bring value to them as you are getting value from them.

There are many ways in which you can approach this issue. For example, you can help by manufacturing the parts to your product in your home country, but assembling the product in the market in which it will be sold. This helps develop the local economy in the developing nation. This will also help you build strong relationships within the community, and people will look out for you.

---

[6] http://www.uschamber.com
[7] http://www.embassyworld.com

I encourage you to go global. I encourage you to get out there and capture your share of that 95% of the world's market that's out there. If you're going to grow your business, if you're going to become a more profitable enterprise, if you're going to expand your horizons, then going global is definitely the way to go.

Conclusion

Going global with your business is not an easy thing to do and can seem like a daunting task to even veteran entrepreneurs. You are up against market entry challenges, environmental challenges, and challenges pertaining to a different business culture, customs, and protocol.

There are people willing to help you though; from your local government to the people with which you will form partnerships to the many different market entry portals available to you. By practicing thorough due diligence, being patient and flexible, you can find success in the global marketplace. And when you do find success, be mindful of the people and the community that helped you achieve it.

Bio of Shelvin D. Longmire

Shelvin D. Longmire is a Washington, DC-based strategic advisor and international consultant specializing in global enterprise management, international business development and market entry strategy, corporate intelligence, and commercial diplomacy and protocol. His areas of expertise also include facilitating international business linkages, joint ventures, and strategic alliances in emerging markets.

Mr. Longmire also serves as the U.S. Director of the Montreal, Canada based international business consultancy and media relations firm, Afrique Expansion, Inc. He has served as a senior project manager with the Northrop Grumman Corporation. Following this, he was the U.S. managing director of an international charter airline that provided customized flights between the U.S., South America, and Europe. And after this, he was vice president of an entrepreneurial information technology and management services firm.

Mr. Longmire serves on the board of the Tri-County International Chamber of Commerce, the African Business Club at the Howard University School of Business, and the American-Nigerian International Chamber of Commerce. His other affiliations include the Center for Global Entrepreneurship and Enterprise Management, the Center for Global Leadership at McDaniel College, and the Academy of International Business.

Mr. Longmire studied political science, international relations, and business management and earned his degree from Troy University. He also holds certifications in Global Business Strategy from Georgetown University and in Global Entrepreneurship from the Thunderbird School of Global Management. He is also an alumnus of the U.S. Foreign Service Institute, the Defense Intelligence College, the Armed Forces Command and Staff College, the U.S. Army Management Engineering College, and the U.S. Air Force Special Operations School.

2

The Going Global on a Dime Process

Going global means different things to different people. International business is simply when individuals or firms conduct a business transaction between different countries. International business is divided into three main areas – income, investment, and trade – according to the International Monetary Fund (IMF)[8].

Income involves return on investment and earnings for creditors, shareholders, and employees. For example, interest payments on debts spanning different countries are income.

Investment involves either direct or portfolio investments. A direct investment is when an investor sets up or acquires, in part or in full, a business in another country. A portfolio investment is investing in financial instruments, either equity or debt.

Trade is when international transactions involve goods or services. Exporting falls within this category. The trading process generally involves three steps: (1) buyer and seller interact before contract, (2) buyer and seller negotiate and sign a contract, and (3) the contract is completed and enforced.

The Going Global on a Dime (GGD) process focuses on doing business in a foreign country more than trade or investment. However, the process and information in this book are still useful for anyone considering any type of foreign transaction.

My experience with going global was the opposite of the path recommended - build domestic capability before considering going global. I packed up and moved to a foreign country to start something new. In truth,

---

[8] http://www.imf.org

there are a lot of pitfalls in this approach, but I quickly learned how to navigate global business opportunities with very few resources. Out of these experiences, and those of others, comes the GGD process.

The GGD process is not about going global and spending no money, but about how to leverage the cash, and other resources, you have to go global. It uses the principle of "use what you have in hand" versus waiting for the windfall that never seems to come.

One of the major reasons small businesses and entrepreneurs give for not going global is not having the money to do so. There has to be a major shift in your mindset, in this regard, for you to tap global markets as an SME or entrepreneur. In most instances, there will never seem to be enough money. Money should be your last consideration for going global, not the first.

In fact, going global is not so much about tapping your own resources, but tapping your resources and those of others. This is what powers your ability to go global.

Another common misconception is that you have to have a successful domestic enterprise before you can go global. While this is good, practical advice because it is something you can leverage, today firms are being born global. That means they go global within two to three years of their creation. Firms are being designed from scratch to take advantage of opportunities wherever they may be found – domestically or globally. This is the framework you want to have for your own enterprise no matter at what stage of development it is.

Admittedly, the going global process is intense, filled with barriers and issues. However, you will find workarounds so that you can go global just as others have done. As with any business venture, you have to be committed, persistent, and innovative.

The first thing you will need to do is a reality check. While there are innumerable opportunities globally, particularly in emerging and frontier markets, you need to know that the process of going global, or being in business globally, is complex. For example, you now need to keep track of laws and regulations in at least two countries.

The best step you can take to start is to get educated about global business issues and the environment. The GGD process focuses on the strategic and practical framework that you can take to go global, not the technical framework or the background. You will find hundreds of sources for this aspect. Three good sources to start are globalEDGE™[9] at Michigan State University, U.S. Export Assistance Centers[10], and local institutions like universities and colleges and chambers of commerce that have international business programs specifically designed for SMEs and entrepreneurs.

After you have gained sufficient knowledge about going global, you then need to assess where you are in terms of readiness. If you are exporting, globalEDGE™ provides the CORE software program, which assesses your organizational and product readiness for exporting. globalEDGE™ may charge a fee, but you can download a similar program from Bradley University's International Business department[11] for free.

You will come away with some basic steps you need to do, such as putting together a company profile and setting up a website. Do as much as recommended that you can, so that you are prepared to do business when the opportunity comes. This only applies if you have an existing business with products and services.

If you are coming up with a new business idea, you will not be able to do as much but you can at least make sure your company is registered, has basic business licenses, and has a bank account. You will, however, have a checklist to refer to in the future as you develop the new business venture.

---

[9] http://globaledge.msu.edu

[10] http://www.export.gov

[11] http://www.bradley.edu/academic/colleges/fcba/centers/turner/established/business/

While this educational process is important, many SMEs and entrepreneurs come away feeling like they have the information, but still cannot go global for various reasons. This is where the GGD process is applied – to help you look at what you have in hand, learn how to move forward to go global with what you have, and implement a first-stage venture abroad.

Before getting into the GGD process though, we need to look at a few key perspectives that will be important to you – unique competitive space, key entrepreneurial tactics, and value creation.

Important Perspectives

There are some perspectives which you will need to understand to put the GGD process to use for you. The first perspective is unique competitive space. Unique competitive space (UCS) is the space for which you are uniquely designed to create value, which inherently gives you a competitive advantage over others. As an entrepreneur, you are wired to succeed in a particular market space. It is your journey to find out what that space is and fully develop it. In fact, there is a UCS for every single person, whether or not he or she chooses to be an entrepreneur.

This insight reveals a shift in a scarcity market mentality to an abundance market mentality and the nature of competition. If everyone has a UCS, this means there must be an abundance of markets to tap. And in your UCS, you are expected to dominate and lead your competition while at the same time work with other people in similar spaces (co-opetition) to leverage opportunities for everyone involved.

So, what does this mean for entrepreneurs in these new paradigms? Let's start with a description of an entrepreneur.

An entrepreneur is a person who creates things based on his or her uniqueness. We are all creators; therefore, we are all entrepreneurs (whether or not we choose to identify with this role).

In business, entrepreneurs create value to create wealth while serving others. The process of creating value starts from the inside (the spirit), then moves to the mind (soul), and then is executed (body). Every good business venture will start with what you create from within you and make tangible. The best business ideas do not start with externalities.

While people are innately creators, or entrepreneurs, they have to choose to live the life of an entrepreneur. This life is a journey not a destination.

Entrepreneurs in this space also understand that making the most of our unique competitive space is more about serving others than ourselves. How well we serve measures our degree of success.

The second perspective is value creation. Every economy is based on the process of creating value, taking a raw resource and transforming it into something of greater value in the eyes of the consumer. For an entrepreneur, this means you take raw components, elements, and knowledge and create unique products and services. When your product or service becomes valuable enough and you offer it at an affordable price to consumers, they will pay you for it (although there are other factors which also come to bear).

The value creation process starts with the business idea, which is a seed planted in your spirit. As you cultivate or nurture these seeds, they become plants. These plants start as sprouts and transform to fully formed plants, e.g., corn. Once the plants have matured, they produce fruit (value) with new seeds (new ideas, business ventures, products, etc.). The new seeds (ideas) produce more plants which produce more fruit (value) and seeds, so multiplication occurs. Multiplication continues until value overflows back to you.

It is the same for a business idea. The idea is transformed into a product or service which people purchase. This leads to more products and services, as well as sales, leading to not just revenue but profit with the right business model.

This analogy also teaches you something important about a new business venture. It cannot produce fruit (value) until it has matured enough. Many entrepreneurs have great ideas but never develop them enough to bring value to customers, so the potential dies on the vine. This is the difficult upfront process any entrepreneurial venture faces. It's important for entrepreneurs to continually re-work the business model to work for the customers and themselves.

The third perspective is key entrepreneurial tactics for taking advantage of the GGD process. The following entrepreneurial tactics are those we have found to help us leverage our opportunities:

- Serve and seed others – help your customers and even other businesses succeed. It helps build the ecosystem you will need to support your own venture.
- Identify and keep your core principles and values – Brian Klemmer offers a good set of core values to follow in the "Compassionate Samurai."
- Live and operate in the abundant entrepreneurial worldview – recognize that there are opportunities out there just for you and pursue them.
- Focus on creating value first, not making money – the flaky financial instruments of the global economic crisis demonstrated why. Things with no value will eventually die out and cause destruction. Money comes as a result of having something of value to exchange.
- Be a warrior – keep at it. You will need to push forward on your own steam; others will not do it for you. Be bold, strategic, relentless, and flexible.
- Use what you have – do not focus on what you don't have. Put to use what you do have.
- Seek knowledge and learn – you will fall behind if you rely on others for your information. Become an expert in your unique competitive space and put it to use.
- Collaborate with others – do not be tempted to go global on your own. Working with others may be a challenge, but it can make your business model much stronger. You become a micro version of a large firm that has its own resources to wield to go global.

- Work on a shoestring budget and stay out of debt – this is called bootstrapping. Guy Kawasaki ("The Art of the Start") and Seth Godin ("The Bootstrapping Bible") provide great insights on how to do this. Use credit facilities for strategic movements like covering expenses until a client with a big order pays.
- Aim at getting clients to start business – don't look for financial assistance to start business. Instead, focus on getting paying customers which ultimately will help prove the market potential of your business.
- Flow with entrepreneurial cycles – the entrepreneurial process ebbs and flows. Learn to act proactively and with urgency, but also learn how to sit back, reflect, and be patient.

Navigating business globally is not just about knowing the context and technical aspects, but how to travel the course like ships sail the seas, which have varying conditions and weather patterns. As with sea travel, there are basic principles that help you work with the variability of going global. The aforementioned perspectives are among them.

Going Global on a Dime Steps

The GGD process is a blueprint for an approximately 18-month process, triggered by completing the aforementioned background preparation. It starts with the mindset that you are going global, but need to find the right opportunities and pathways that fit your strengths and situation. You also know that your success is tied to not only the strengths you possess, but strengths of others into which you can tap.

There are four steps you will do simultaneously and iteratively. The first is identifying opportunities. This involves scanning the environment while brainstorming business ideas with the knowledge you possess.

The second step is to gain knowledge about the business environment in which you will be working. You need to understand the markets, laws and regulations, competition, barriers, incentives, etc.

The third step is to recognize and leverage your strengths to take advantage of business opportunities. There are strengths of which we typically think, e.g., skills, knowledge, and physical assets. However, there are other assets like relationships and goodwill for which you need to account.

The fourth step is to develop the ecosystem that will support the success of the global venture from suppliers to distributors to partners to consumers. The ecosystem is not just the supply chain, or value chain. A key component of your ecosystem could be a person who is able to open doors for you to get to a key resource you need. The person isn't in your value chain, but is key in getting a resource you need for the value chain.

The focus of this step is partnerships. Through these partnerships, you are able to add the strength of others to your cadre of strengths for a particular business venture. This is an extension of the second step in which you leverage your own strengths – you now leverage the strength of others.

After you flow with these first four steps, there will come a point at which you need to begin the funneling process, narrowing down and executing one or a few opportunities. The fifth step that begins the funneling phase is prioritizing and choosing a few suitable opportunities.

The sixth step is to develop business models and concept documents for the opportunities chosen. The business model demonstrates the viability of the venture at a strategic level. It shows what you will produce and sell, who you will sell it to, what it will take to operate, partnerships and channels you will use, the cost of operation, etc. The concept document is the written explanation of the business model in three to five pages.

The seventh step is to execute legal documentation and agreements, as well as develop an implementation plan for the first stage (which is approximately a year in length). And the eighth and final step is to implement and evaluate.

One final note about the GGD process, it looks at your going global pursuit as a project not as a formal business structure. You do not want to get into too much formality or infrastructure early on as you will need flexibility to move and configure your resources. You will be executing a proof-of-concept project, which essentially helps you refine and finalize your business model for the global opportunity while limiting risk and containing costs. By focusing on things on a smaller scale, you can work out many of the issues that are associated with running the business venture and build the relationships and partnerships you will need in the long run.

Conclusion

Your first task is to get educated about global business so you understand the dynamics at play. You can certainly pursue specific opportunities, but it is important not to neglect the basics.

Preparation and planning are critical to your success. However, you should not prepare and plan so much that you forsake implementation. I think it is better to prepare and plan a general framework upfront, then adapt your plan and prepare some more as you move along.

Keep in mind that throughout this whole process you should continually be doing research on all fronts – the country, the sector and market, business opportunities, potential partnerships. You start by casting your net wide, then narrow as you are able to see a path to take an opportunity.

3

Opportunities and the Business Environment

The GGD process starts with identifying opportunities. This involves scanning the environment. The best market opportunities are those that start with fulfilling a need. For example, in emerging markets basic services, e.g., housing, transport, food, water, education, and health, are inadequate for the demand.

Before discussing this step, let's reflect on what an opportunity is. An opportunity is a possibility due to a favorable combination of circumstances. The combination of favorable circumstances includes the strengths you and your partners bring to the business venture. In fact, the strengths help create the favorable circumstances.

If we align our understanding of opportunity with the entrepreneurial perspectives shared in the previous chapter, you will find the following quotes about opportunity insightful, and perhaps a few might be entertaining:

- "We are all faced with a series of great opportunities brilliantly disguised as impossible situations." *Charles Swindoll*
- "Luck is what happens when preparation meets opportunity." *Seneca, Ancient Roman Philosopher*
- "Don't wait for extraordinary opportunities. Seize common occasions and make them great. Weak men wait for opportunities; strong men make them." *Orison Swett Marden*
- "Opportunity is missed by most people because it is dressed in overalls and looks like work." *Thomas Alva Edison*

Looking at Opportunities

Some people have an innate sense for seeing an opportunity, but most of us have to be trained to recognize business opportunities. A simple framework for identifying opportunities is MADE – market, assembly (or manufacturing), distribution (or agent), and existing business.

Market refers to taking advantage of specific market, or demand-driven, opportunities. Assembly refers to producing products by either manufacturing them or assembling components into a final product. Distribution refers to becoming an agent or distributor of someone else's products or services. And, existing business refers to leveraging the business you already have.

For market opportunities, you can use the following questions to help you identify them in a foreign market:

- Is there a market gap or shortage?
- Can you transfer an idea or concept from one industry to another?
- Can you invent a new service or product?
- Can you create value for customers from people who have under-utilized skills?
- Can you take advantage of a growth trend or create your own market demand?
- Are there circumstances, e.g., market switch (CD to MP3 players) that you can take advantage of?
- Is there a product that has failed in a certain context, but you can make successful in your space?
- Can you take advantage of fashions, fads, or growth trends?
- Is there a niche market you can serve?

For assembly or manufacturing opportunities, you can use the following questions to help you identify them in a foreign market:

- Is there research and development IP that you can commercialize?
- Will someone allow you to manufacture and market their product abroad under license?
- Can you improve an existing product or service?
- Can you replace imports into the foreign market, e.g., assembling the product locally which may bring down cost of the product?

- Can you recycle products and/or handle waste materials and byproducts?
- Can you assemble products or combine components?
- Can you add value to or substitute materials in existing products?

For distribution opportunities, you can use the following questions to help you identify them in a foreign market:

- For which products or services would you be a good agent or distributor?
- Would you like to serve as an intermediary – an import or export agent?
- Are you able to help someone expand their market areas?

For existing business opportunities, you can ask the following questions to help you identify them in a foreign market:

- What existing businesses could you buy and operate?
- Can you buy a franchise or franchise your own business?
- What aspects of your existing business are you not utilizing that you could activate?
- What spinoffs can you develop from your current business?
- What opportunities arise because of your current business?

There is another element to identifying opportunities that I need to emphasize. Look for the opportunities that are right around you, even for global opportunities. You don't have to search far and wide often to find opportunities of which you can take advantage. For example, find local domestic manufacturers for whom you can serve as an agent to enter a foreign market or serve as an export agent.

Every opportunity has rewards and risks. You will need to determine for yourself whether the rewards outweigh the risks. Generally, the highest rewards have the highest risks. However, you can learn to mitigate risks based on how you structure your business model and operations.

A good balance to start with your first going global project is to identify a project that will give you sufficient rewards with a level of risk that you are willing to take on. It's not always the projects that start off big that win, but those that start small and grow and evolve – a seed becoming a tree, then the tree becoming an orchard. The success of Facebook over the last five years is an example.

Looking at the Business Environment

Looking at the business environment and issues you may have to face is a major research task on your part, or on the part of someone you partner with or pay to help you. For every issue you face in a domestic market, you have the same in other markets and more. This is where SMEs and entrepreneurs can get bogged down in the technical details of going global. It is a reality you cannot get around, but doing adequate research will help you navigate this complex facet of going global.

One note, your research will only provide you general guidance. You should expect that you will need to validate information and consult with professionals for your particular situation. However, doing your own background research can help you ask more intelligent questions and leverage the money you are investing in professional services.

When you look at the business environment, you first want to consider macro variables – variables that affect a country and its market. However, you will also want to review global, regional, and local variables that may impact the environment in which you will operate. For example, if you operate in the European Union (EU) even though member nations are sovereign, certain EU laws may supersede laws in the country in which you choose to operate.

Regent University's Center for Entrepreneurship outlines (Appendix B) several areas you want to research. These areas include general country background (e.g., geography, people, economy), structural factors (e.g., government, rule of law, fiscal policy), international trade, financial and capital markets, social and cultural factors, industry and sector development, human capital, technological innovation and research, foreign direct investment, infrastructure development, and the forecast for the country. While all of this information is not in one place, you will be surprised to find that you can get a good background profile with few monetary resources.

If you know one or a few countries that you would like to explore, you can collect an enormous amount of information from under ten sources. If you concentrate on this task for a week, you will get a better picture of the landscape quickly. These are the sources to start with as most of the information is free or costs little:

- Country's official website – This includes the major portal for the government, department of trade and industry, department of planning/economic development, and any departments focused on the sector in which you are interested.

- Regional development banks – For emerging and developing regions, there are regional banks like the African Development Bank (ADB).[12] Regional banks work closely with the member countries in their regions so they are the next closest set of institutions to the countries themselves. They keep track of major projects, initiatives, and funding in the region. You can learn a lot about development and infrastructure through them.

- International Monetary Fund (IMF) – The IMF is the international institution which tracks the macroeconomic situation in most countries around the world. They do economic updates on each country at least every two years.

- Chambers of commerce and industry – I have already alluded to the usefulness of chambers of commerce in the country in which you are interested. At times though, you will need to do a lot of follow up by phone in order to get to the information you seek. If you visit the country, it will obviously be a lot easier to get access to the information they have available. You will also want to check if there are chambers from your country established in the country of interest, or a bi-lateral chamber, e.g., U.S.-Angola Chamber of Commerce.

---

[12] http://www.afdb.org

- Diplomatic missions[13] – Speak with both your country's embassy in the country of interest and the country of interest's embassy in your country, if possible. They will be able to point you to many different sources of information and people who can assist you.
- Culture Grams[14] – These four-page briefs offer you high-level insight into a country's overall culture. They are great for background information and the information is validated with natives from the country covered. If you live in the United States, you can find them at your local library and access them for free. You can also buy a culture gram for a particular country for under $5.00 online.
- International trade sources – First, start with international trade resources offered by your home country. In the United States, the place to start is the U.S. Export website as mentioned before. Libraries in the United States also have access to several major trade statistics platforms. Check with the reference desk in the library. The World Trade Organization (WTO) also develops trade policy reviews[15] about every three to five years for countries around the world. A review highlights the conditions for trade in a country.

If you do not have any particular countries in which you are interested, I suggest a different path as there are just too many countries to try to look at all at once. Here are a few suggestions:

1. Identify countries with which your country has trade agreements and which speak your native tongue.
2. Identify countries that have an embassy in your country with a commercial liaison and where your country has an embassy. The countries in steps 1 and 2 should be similar.

---

[13] Check with your foreign affairs or state department to find foreign embassies in your home country or your country's embassies in other countries.
[14] http://www.culturegrams.com
[15] http://www.wto.org/english/tratop_e/tpr_e/tpr_e.htm

3. Check out market research readily available on the list of countries you have. Even if you don't live in the United States[16] or the United Kingdom[17], you can access the market research and doing business guides they have prepared on many countries around the world for their citizens. You just need to be aware that the content is written for their audiences, so you will need to reframe it, depending on your country of origin.
4. Begin to check out pathways to connect you to those markets. This is both online and offline research, but the key is to identify the people and organizations that can be leveraged to help you enter markets of interest. Your focus is looking at potential partners.

As you are doing your research, you will likely find discrete opportunities that have pathways to entering a particular market that you could use and are not tied to the process you have been following. You will need to build a background profile for the countries in which those opportunities arise if they are not already included in your research.

After you have developed background profiles, you will need to consider the practical issues of doing business or trade globally, but in your specific context. You will want to ask, "How do these things apply in my specific situation?"

I have prepared a list of questions (Appendix C) that I ponder at different times in the GGD process. You will find these and the list provided by Regent University useful in your research process, which really is a continual process throughout the life of your going global venture. They help you ask more intelligent questions of you and others, as well as help you interface with professionals you might hire to help in your research and strategy more effectively.

The one mistake I find very typical with people going global is that they do not do enough of their own upfront research to truly get a feel for

[16] Market research reports done by U.S. government can be accessed through http://www.export.gov.
[17] Market research reports done by the U.K. Trade and Investment Office can be accessed at http://www.ukti.gov.uk/export/countries.html by country.

the dynamics at play. So, spend some time making inquiries and doing research. You won't get all the answers at once or in one place, but you will have better data to make informed decisions.

Conclusion

You can see that the Going Global on a Dime process is designed specifically for doing business in a foreign market. This process can be effective whether you already have an established business or your business is going to be born globally. The GGD process is designed to help you leverage not only your cash and assets but the cash and assets of other people as well.

Study up on the way that business is conducted in your country of interest and how their economy works. Spend time gathering and going over as much information about the country, its people, and their customs. This research will prove to be invaluable when you enter your foreign market.

4

Managing Intellectual Property

William Northcote

Whether starting a company or developing a product, anywhere in the world, you always need to make sure your ideas are well protected. All business relationships involve risk, but by taking the proper steps, you can assure yourself that if something goes awry, the law is on your side.

Intellectual property (IP) is a collection of legal rights that protect the creative work of individuals, although IP can obviously become owned by corporations. These rights recognize the intellectual efforts of creators, which gives them protection to allow them to commercialize and profit from their work for different periods of time, depending on the nature of the work.

If you invest time and money into an innovation, the first step to protecting it is to determine the ways that it can be ripped off, replicated, or stolen. It is also important to identify those people who would most likely do this, and then devise a strategy to prevent it from happening. As great as your idea may be, it is of little monetary value to you in the hands of someone else who doesn't pay royalties or other compensation.

The most important thing to do early on is to make sure your innovation is legally protected. You need to establish some form, or multiple forms, of IP protection. IP protection can include trademarks, copyrights, patents, trade secrets, and industrial designs.

Trademark

A trademark is a name, word, phrase, logo, symbol, design, image, or a combination of these elements that identifies the source or qualities of a product or service. Trademarks can be registered or unregistered, although a registered trademark offers much more protection.

If you decide to use an unregistered or common law trademark, there is no guarantee that you will be the only person who is able to use the logo and name you created. Common law dictates that the owner of an unregistered trademark is legally protected from other people using it only in the geographical areas where it is used.

If you register your trademark, you obtain a statutory monopoly for the trademark in association with the products or services listed in your registration. This ensures that nobody else in your country of registration can legally use your logo, thus protecting the brand name and reputation. Trademarks are nationally based, so if you plan to take your product, service, or company global, you must obtain trademarks for each country where you operate.

Your product or services can dictate the countries where you should file for a trademark. For example, if you're making snow skis, you probably don't need to worry about obtaining a trademark in Jamaica.

If finances are constrained, you should determine which countries are your most important markets or the markets in which your products or services are produced or created. You can then focus your IP strategy on those markets. For example, if you are producing a product for distribution in North America, you should seek protection in Canada, the United States, and perhaps Mexico. But if it's being manufactured in China, you should get a trademark registration there, because in some circumstances, your manufacturer can gain trademark rights even though you've contracted for them to manufacture for you.

It is also very important that you use your trademark after getting it. In most countries, if you apply for and obtain a trademark and don't actually use it within a specified period of time (this varies from country to country), you can lose your rights to the trademark. In other words, you need to use it fairly frequently in order to avoid getting expunged for what is called "non-use."

One common trademark mistake entrepreneurs make is in working with graphic artists. For example, if you hire someone to design your logo, it is important to have them sign the IP rights over to you. You have to literally purchase the intellectual property rights in the underlying design. It is a simple, though often overlooked, procedure that can save you from potential legal hassles down the road. You can also have an upfront contractor agreement, which stipulates that any design work done for you is your intellectual property.

Copyright

Trademarks and copyrights are often confused with one another. A trademark is a word or logo that protects the goodwill in goods and services. A copyright is a statutory right that protects the expression of an idea.

While trademarks are protected on a national level, copyrights are recognized in most developed countries in the world, because of a series of international treaties. If you are a resident of a country that is part of this treaty system, then you have copyright protection in the other countries even though you take no formal steps to record it.[18]

A copyright can be used to protect a wide range of unique works that you create for a limited period of time, in exchange for public disclosure of your work. It can subsist in books, short stories, plays, sheet music, dramatic works, maps, paintings, photographs, architectural drawings, sound recordings, motion pictures, and computer programs. Copyrights are not based on artistic or literary merit, so however rough your idea may be, you can still copyright it.

Unlike trademarks, copyrights are usually not registered. You can register copyrights, but there's no requirement that you do so. In fact, it's seldom done. It is good practice to place a copyright notice on all your products. This can be simply done by adding the copyright symbol (©) or by writing: Copyright 2011 [Your Name] - All rights reserved.

---

[18] The World Intellectual Property Organization (WIPO) is the coordinating body for international treaties and information on which countries are members to a particular treaty is available on WIPO's website - http://www.wipo.int.

Patents

A patent is a statutory monopoly that protects an invention, and in some cases, protects the expression of the idea. There are really three criteria you must demonstrate in order to obtain a patent. First, it must show novelty (be the first in the world). Second, it must show utility (be functional and operative). Third, it must show inventive ingenuity and not be obvious to someone skilled in that area. Inventions can be products (e.g., a tire pump), a composition (e.g., a chemical composition used in lubricants for tire pumps), an apparatus (e.g., a machine for making tire pumps), a process (e.g., method for making tire pumps) or an improvement on any of these.

A patent allows you to prevent others from making, using, or selling your invention in each country where a patent is granted from the day that your patent is granted for a prescribed length of time. In Canada, this length of time is limited to 20 years. In exchange for this protection, you must provide a full description of the invention so everyone can benefit from this advance in technology and knowledge.

When you file a patent, you need to find a patent agent with a background in the field pertaining to your invention. The person needs to understand the invention, in the context of development in the field, and must develop a patent application that reflects the technical background.

An important thing to consider before your patent is finalized is if the patent is broad enough to prevent others from taking the idea. After your patent is granted, the idea is out there for the rest of world to see, and if you have a great idea, people are going to try and make it better. Over 90% of patents granted are for the improvement of an existing patented invention.

Industrial Design

An industrial design consists of the creation of a shape, configuration, or composition of pattern or color, or even a combination of pattern and color in three-dimensional form containing aesthetic value. An industrial design can be a two- or three-dimensional pattern used to produce a product, industrial commodity, or handicraft. Industrial design protection is essentially the protection of the appearance of the goods.

A good example is the old fashioned Coca-Cola bottle with the hourglass shape; it is a unique industrial design. You can register designs, which is relatively straightforward, but that doesn't afford as much protection as a patent. In the case of the Coca-Cola bottle, there's no utility to it and the design serves no function. It's just decorative and, therefore, is ineligible for a patent.

Trade Secrets

The final form of IP protection involves trade secrets. This is simply protecting your intellectual property by keeping it a secret. A trade secret is really anything that is inherently valuable. It is generally not known, or reasonably ascertainable to the public or even competition within the same industry. It gives the owner an economic or competitive advantage and can include any formula, practice, design, pattern, device, or compilation of information.

Sticking with the Coca-Cola theme, an example of a trade secret is the beverage recipe. It is not patented because, after a predetermined number of years, patents become public knowledge and anyone can have access to them.

Of course, it is of paramount importance that you protect your trade secrets. Typically, you do that by having confidentiality agreements. Sometimes these are imposed by the nature of the legal relationship and sometimes by contract, or both. For important trade secrets, you want to have both. For example, your engineering staff will have written agreements that provide for non-disclosure and the ownership of trade secrets.

Trade secrets can be broken down into four different categories: specific product information (e.g., chemical formulas), technological secrets (e.g., "know-how" or "show-how" knowledge of a process or methodology which others have not yet developed), strategic business information (e.g., customer lists), and specialized compilations of information.

Choosing Who Has Access to Your IP

Once you have your product ready for market, you need people to help you manufacture, market, and sell it. It is critical that you choose wisely when selecting partners. This includes employees, distributors, customers, and end users.

Even with all the legal paperwork negotiated and signed, you cannot prevent someone from attempting to rip off your product, but you do have power to choose with whom you work. Partner selection is perhaps the most important thing of all.

In some areas of the world, people want to develop a personal relationship before forming a business relationship. It is ideal to partner with someone on a smaller project before going into a large joint venture or strategic alliance. We sometimes refer to this process as, "letting the clients date before they get married."

One of the most important things is to try and structure your business relationships so that the licensee, the person using your intellectual property, is motivated to do the right thing. Frankly, the last thing you want to do is litigate in court to preserve your rights.

You want to create a structure that will motivate the licensee to do what he or she should do. That's particularly important in jurisdictions where there is less emphasis on the formal legal contract and more on the personal relationship.

North Americans and Europeans tend to be very contract-focused, whereas Asians are much more focused on the relationship. It's important to recognize emphasis is placed differently in various parts of the world. So, you should find a way to work together that addresses both concerns.

There are some very important contractual terms that you should include in all partnership contracts. In a supply chain situation, you can require that the licensee only has the ability to purchase the product through specific distributors. This enables you to do two things. One, it allows you to control the supply, so if there is a legal fight, it is possible contractually to have the right to cut off the supply. This means they can't continue manufacturing because they can't get some critical elements.

Two, which is quite common in the fast-food industry, it allows you to verify that your licensee or franchisee is actually reporting their revenues and profits properly, and paying the proper amount. Most food franchisees are required to buy their food products from designated suppliers. So, franchisors have direct access to some aspects of franchisees' financial records, and know how much product is purchased.

A second critical provision is a contractual right by the licensor to audit the books and records of the licensee. It would also be wise to include a provision that any material underreporting results in the counterparty paying the audit costs. These provisions need to be carefully considered on a case-by-case basis. Most importantly, you should strive to create a relationship with your counterparty where they are motivated for good business reasons to perform as agreed, rather than rely on contractual obligations.

Intellectual Property Management Basics

Once you have an invention or new idea from which you want to profit, you should take steps to safeguard your IP. First, undertake a detailed risk management analysis. Define how your idea can be compromised by others and identify whom those culprits might be. Decide if there are any legal steps you need to take to prevent this from happening, such as obtaining a trademark or patent.

Remember to develop strong contractual and business relationships with your partners and employees to minimize your chances of being ripped off. Remember that partner selection is perhaps the most critical decision to make. It is important to first spend some time together, and gain an understanding of the local market.

Do not overlook the importance of registering trademarks. When money is tight, you may think you are better served spending it elsewhere and not registering your trademarks at the outset. Unfortunately, when that happens, registration of the trademark is often forgotten and you lose a good portion of your legal protection.

If you plan to take your business global, it is important to remember that it may take longer than you anticipate for all the paperwork. If you plan on doing business in a foreign country six months from now, you should start filling out and submitting the paperwork now. First start with the countries you will be dealing with directly and work from there. This way you will not be held up when you are ready to do business.

And in a worse-case scenario, if you are ripped off, take legal action. This will not only help to minimize damages, it will also help develop a reputation that you are prepared to fight to protect your rights.

Handling Intellectual Property Infringement

Some people and organizations make stealing other people's IP their business. For example, you can watch movies that are still in theaters from a website, or the guy selling fake Rolexes out of a briefcase. If you can't get the violator to stop the infringing behavior without resorting to litigation, you often end up in court.

In this case, you want to seek interim relief, which is effectively a court remedy before you go to trial. In the U.S., it is called a temporary restraining order. In some countries, it's called an injunction.

In order to get the relief, there is also variability in what you must demonstrate to the court. In Canada and England, you have to show that there is a serious issue and there will be irreparable harm if you don't get your injunction. Irreparable harm means something that money alone will not satisfy. For example, in a trademark case, the allegation might be, "They're distributing goods with my trademark on them and are damaging my reputation because they're selling shoddy goods. That will damage my reputation and there's really no way that money can make up for that."

The other test is that there has to be a balance of convenience. In other words, it is more convenient that they do it now rather than wait.

The entire proceedings, especially if things go to court, can vary from country to country. This requires that you have good local representation.

If you end up in court by filing a law suit, you can potentially collect damages arising from an infringement of your IP. Depending on the type of IP which was infringed, your financial reward in damages and the way that the violation is remedied will vary.

If a clear violation is established, you may be entitled to all the profits earned by the guilty party, along with the option to destroy or keep the goods in question. This is called an infringement remedy and, in exceptional cases, can result in punitive damages.

If your compromised IP is protected by a copyright, you can get an interdiction. This is an order from the court that prevents the offending product from entering the market in the country where the copyright was established.

IP is a complex area of law and your legal rights and remedies depend on your factual circumstances and the jurisdiction. The foregoing is a brief summary of the law, and is not intended to be legal advice. You should always consult counsel for specific advice.

Conclusion

Your intellectual property is the heart and soul of your unique business and it is paramount that you do everything that you can to protect it. Look into trademarks, copyrights, and patents and use them. Money may be tight initially with a new company but the money you spend protecting your IP is money well spent.

You will need to partner with someone to be successful in international business, but choose your partners wisely and get to know them on a personal level before doing business together, if it is possible. Do not jump into a joint venture with your partner, start small and work towards your main goals. Make sure that your partners sign agreements that specifically protect your IP and do not be afraid to take legal action if your IP becomes compromised.

Bio of William Northcote

Bill Northcote is Chair of Shibley Righton LLP's business law practice group and the firm's resident expert on international law. With expertise in mergers and acquisitions, divestitures, and financing, he has 29 years of experience and a strong academic background. His areas of practice include business law, technology, and intellectual property law. He currently serves on the boards of a number of clients from various industries.

Bill has an LL.M. (International Business Law) from Osgoode Hall Law School, an LL.B. (cum laude) from the University of Ottawa, and a Bachelor of Arts (Economics and History) from the University of Toronto. While in law school he served as a member of the Board of Editors of the Ottawa Law Review. He is the author of a number of published legal articles on such topics as Cultural Industries under the Free Trade Agreement, International Commercial Arbitration, Software Law and Equipment Leasing, and is also author of a chapter on Canada for the book 'Media, Advertising and Entertainment Law Throughout the World'.

An aficionado of photography, blues and roots music, and international travel, Bill has taught at York University in Toronto and at Nankai University in Tianjin, China. In addition, he was an instructor in the Law Society of Upper Canada's Bar Admission Course for more than ten years. He is a member of the Canadian Bar Association and Canadian Tax Foundation, and sits on the Board of Directors of MultiLaw, which is an association of law firms in 56 countries around the world.

William L. Northcote
Partner
SHIBLEY RIGHTON LLP
250 University Avenue, Suite 700
Toronto, Ontario M5H 3E5
T: 416.214.5252
F: 416.214.5452
E: Bill.Northcote@shibleyrighton.com
W: www.shibleyrighton.com

5

Due Diligence

Lauri Elliott
Joseph Price

Due diligence is essentially you trying to get to know as much about a specific business, business market, or partner as you can. As Warren Buffett once said, "Never invest in a business you cannot understand."

Due diligence is a method to minimize risk and increase likelihood of expected outcomes. There are both formal and informal ways to conduct due diligence, and when dealing with emerging or frontier markets both pathways are typically necessary.

In the context of due diligence, there are different levels. They are buyer-seller (transaction) relationships with single or large purchases, partnerships, and investments.

Transaction Due Diligence

In international trade, there is a transaction between a buyer and seller. The buyer expects to get goods as specified while the seller expects to receive payment for those goods. Buyer and seller interaction starts with each party searching for the other. The buyer will search channels, including business networks, the Internet, etc., to find a seller for the product or service he or she desires, whereas the seller will make sure that he or she can be found by potential buyers. In the process, both the buyer and seller may learn more about trading between countries.

As the buyer and seller seriously consider completing a contract, there may be samples provided and references requested on both sides. In larger or long-term transactions, buyers and sellers may meet face to face – the buyer may visit the seller's facilities, for example.

Contract negotiations involve providing details on product or service specifications, price, and quality. Also, time and place for delivery and form and time of payment are agreed upon.

When the contract is ready to be signed, both buyer and seller should institute precautions like having payment intermediaries – e.g., an escrow account, a letter of credit, or even PayPal. They should also consider insurance against non-payment or non-performance, if available.

And finally, if the contract is signed and completed but something doesn't work out, buyers and sellers have to consider how to collect on and/or remedy the contract. This may lead to mediation, litigation, or insurance claims.

Banks, finance brokers, and governments have different tools available for trade transactions. Check with your government agencies involved with trade to see what resources they have and large commercial banks. In the United States, the U.S. EXIM Bank[19] is a great source with which to start. The U.S. International Trade Administration has prepared a guide for U.S. exporters to understand the trade transaction process and instruments available.[20]

The level of due diligence for transactions depends on the amount of the transaction. It is wise to do basic due diligence to at least verify the identity and credibility of the buyer or seller. As a buyer, you want to be assured that you will get the product you asked for. As the seller, you want to be assured you get paid and that the good or service you are providing will be used in way that is a positive reflection of your company.

Entrepreneurs, who are sellers, often think that because a transaction is cash there is no need for due diligence. It is still important to verify customers to make sure there is no legal reason not to sell to them, e.g., they are from a sanctioned country, involved in sanctioned actions, or are sanctioned themselves.

---

[19] http://www.exim.gov
[20] http://trade.gov/media/publications/pdf/trade_finance_guide2007.pdf

The first source for getting information is the Internet. While this is more useful in developed markets, it has served me well even in developing markets. I almost always "Google" a company or person to see what is being said about them online. This is considered a secondary source of information, so primary sources of information, which provide facts on the company, e.g., company registration or financial records, are also needed.

The U.S. EXIM Bank has identified basic information it will look for when considering transactions for funding. The information it chooses to collect is a baseline set of data you should consider collecting in any type of going global venture – trade (transaction), partnership, or investment of any significance. Here is the information to collect:

- Name, address, and history of entity
- Legal status and date of establishment (Is the entity in good standing in the country of origin or operation?)
- Description of business activity
- Number of employees and status within industry
- Trade references, commercial morality, and pay history
- Financial standing

There are companies that will do credit checks, which can be an important step, for sellers in transactions. The U.S. EXIM Bank maintains a list of firms that do so in almost any country in the world.[21]

There are other channels that can help you build a background profile of the company with which you plan to do business. Check with your embassy in the country of the company, as well as the embassy of the country in your home country. Also, contact local chambers of commerce to learn more about the company on the ground.

---

[21] http://www.exim.gov/pub/ins/pdf/eib99-08.pdf

Partnership Due Diligence

You will have noticed that I place a lot of emphasis on the power of partnerships and networks to being successful at going global. No matter how many "systems" we come up with, they still center on people interactions or supporting them. We are not moving into an age where relationships will matter less, but they will matter more in global business.

In my view, business success is tied to relationship success with consumers, suppliers, partners, etc. Strong healthy relationships help you leverage better and bigger opportunities, so how you handle them is important.

In my own experience, the Western over reliance on contract frameworks hampers positive relationship growth and opportunities. Even when things go bad, good partnerships can work through the issues in or outside of contract boundaries. You can do business successfully without contracts, but you cannot do business successfully without relationships.

Having said that, building relationships does not mean you forsake due diligence. In fact, you will find that they go hand in hand. Due diligence is part of the "dating" period before companies enter long-term partnerships. The goal of due diligence, as mentioned before, is to find out as much about the business and partner as you can so you can determine if they suit you.

It is more common these days for your counterparts to be familiar with typical agreements, e.g., non-disclosure, service level, and memorandums of understanding, as they engage with business transactions across borders. So, the fact that you need to do due diligence, which may include, requesting official documentation and facts, is not an issue. However, the way in which you do it may be. For example, it might be offensive to some business people in developing nations to ask for business information upfront. Not that they are not willing to give it, but it is the context in which it is acquired.

You can find gracious ways of doing due diligence. For example, you will find that if you meet (virtually or face-to-face) and have conversations with potential partners that you will get most of the basic information you need, e.g., address, business activities, number of employees. Instead of framing your conversation with demands for information, focus on learning about and showing interest in the potential partner. Congenial conversation can go a long way.

When larger risks are involved, it is advisable to visit, meet, and observe the potential partner in their natural setting. This affords you the opportunity to collect due diligence information informally and build personal relationships.

At the end of the day, you will still need the appropriate information to make informed decisions about the potential partnership. So, in addition to the basic background information, you should collect information that will help you answer the following questions:

- What are the market risks?
- What are the technology risks?
- What are the alliance implementation risks?
- What are the operational risks?

Not only do you want to understand the risks, you want to know if you can mitigate or minimize them.

Investment Due Diligence
by Joseph Price

Investment due diligence is simply the process by which a potential investor evaluates and becomes better acquainted with a potential investment in order to get a better understanding of the risks and rewards that the investment offers. When conducted correctly, due diligence offers potential investors the opportunity to act with higher levels of confidence and can be the difference between profitability and loss. Different investors have varying expectations for risk and returns, both social and financial. An investment that's perfect for one group isn't necessarily a good fit for another, so it's a very subjective business.

Due diligence, as a term, can often be considered intimidating. In reality, it couldn't be further from that. Generally, the only time due diligence is cast in a negative light is when it has not been done thoroughly enough and something important gets missed. In fact, due diligence is not only a positive, it is a necessity. If you are going to make a decision with a significant amount of money at stake, you want your decision to be as informed as possible.

As with any business venture or transaction, the scale of it will determine the type and rigor of due diligence. However, in investment cases, you need to lay out your objectives and parameters. The following are some questions you should ask yourself:

- How much are you looking to invest?
- How long are you intending to hold the investment?
- What type of investment are you looking to make?
- Can you work with the culture of the people that are there?
- How much of the company do you want to own?
- What social and/or environmental impacts do you hope your investments will have?
- How do you achieve your goals?

You may notice that these questions are similar to those you need to answer if you were starting a business yourself.

Also, if you are the owner of the company and trying to get people to invest in it, you have to do your own investigation as well. The following are some questions for which you should get answers about investors:

- Does the other party actually have the money to go through with the deal?
- If they are paying in stock, what's the record of the stock?
- If you have employees, how are they going to be treated?
- Are the corporate cultures compatible?
- How will they treat your customers?
- Would you be proud to be associated with this company/person? What's their reputation?

For investment due diligence, there are three different types of due diligence used to assess risk. They are legal, financial, and market.

It is especially crucial to understand the extent of the company's obligations. This is where legal due diligence is almost invaluable. You need to understand what potential losses are, warranties, leases, employee contracts, compensation arrangements, etc. Because of the nature of this type of due diligence, I recommend having an attorney handle it.

Financial due diligence is really about understanding the target company's, or potential investment's, financial health. This involves reviewing a company's financial needs:

- What are the objectives?
- What pieces need to be analyzed, e.g., stock option plan?
- What is the company's monthly earning rate?
- If not profitable, when does the manager expect it to be?
- How fast are sales growing?
- How does the business model relate to each element of the budget?

Market due diligence is really about dissecting a company's, or investment's, position in its industry. Some questions to consider are:

- Who are its competitors? How does the company compete?
- Who is the company using to get its product or service out to the public?
- Who are its channel partners?
- What is the industry, of which the company is a part, like?
- What are other companies in this field selling for? How are they performing?
- How is the management?
- Are these people with whom you will be able to work?
- How successful have they been?
- Who are the buyers and suppliers?
- What is the buying power of the customer?
- What products and services are offered?
- Are they reaching the customers they should?
- What are the strengths of the customer base?
- Does the product or service address an actual need?
- Is there room for expansion of the products or services into new markets?

- How does the company generate money?
- Is the business model built for making money for the long haul or is it capitalizing on a current trend?
- What are the problems with the company? (Things that keeps the owner up at night.)

If done correctly, due diligence costs should be directly proportional to the size of the investment (money wise). So, the larger the project the larger the cost is for due diligence.

Keep in mind that even when it seems that all of the cards are in your favor, there is an inherent risk in any business. If you are sinking your life's savings into your project, be sure that you are fully aware of the risk that you are taking, nothing is guaranteed.

Business is a funny thing and there are outliers. There are some businesses that have a tough road to climb; no matter how much effort is being put in, things just do not seem to be working out. Then, there are others where all of the stars align and they blow up overnight.

Keep in mind that the bottom line before investing in something is that your goal is to obtain something of value. Don't let yourself fall in love with a loser because you like one aspect of what they are offering. Make sure, through your due diligence, that you are backing a winner.

For those without very much experience, make sure you are working with people who have had a lot of success and are able to point out red flags before you make a poor decision. These people will also be able to find the little things that you may overlook and could turn into potential gold mines.

Due diligence is what we would do most likely anyway before investing in something, for emerging markets sometimes you just need to get a little creative about how you gather your information. When focusing on international investments, whether small or large, you can rely on local chambers of commerce[22] to help you with understanding the environment and market of that particular industry in the country in which you are interested. A chamber can serve as a secondary source.

However, as mentioned before in this chapter, it is important that you get some direct input. It is important that you talk to a customer, partner, employee, or someone who deals with the company in which you are interested so you can feel out how the company operates and is viewed.

So, where else can you turn to find out even more? There are quite a few companies and firms that specialize in doing market research and due diligence in foreign markets that you can turn to. If not, try and partner with someone that already lives in that country, who is familiar with the language, the market, and how business is conducted there. Talk to people, you may be surprised as to what you can learn.

It often seems that in the world of investing the old saying rings true, the greater the risk the greater the reward. If you have done the necessary due diligence, you can cut down on your risk, but not all situations are ideal. Be aware of fraud when making deals with partners that you have never and may never meet. If a deal sounds too good to be true, it probably is.

It is always ideal to work with a partner on smaller deals before you start throwing around a lot of money. By offering this option, it will also help to weed out potential frauds or opportunities that will not pan out for you.

Also, time has a way of revealing potential issues, so there is no need to rush. Especially in developing countries, there are literally thousands of business opportunities of which you can take advantage. Even if you do not end up entering an investment in which you were initially interested, you can still take away the knowledge that you gained through your due diligence and apply it to another opportunity.

Building mutual, trusting, and strong relationships is essential. They can only help your cause.

---

[22] The World Chambers Federation maintains a directory of chambers of commerce in most countries at http://chamberdirectory.worldchambers.com.

Another option to help mitigate risk is to look into becoming a co-op entrepreneur where you can partner with one or more entrepreneurs who are in the same position as you are. There are a lot of people in the United States, and other countries around the world, that are looking into investing in foreign markets. A partnership like this will be beneficial for all involved parties for a variety of reasons. First and foremost, you will not have to invest as much money as you would if you were doing it alone. This is also a way that, through partnership with a few people, you can make a larger investment overall.

Second, and equally as important, you will have more sets of intelligent eyes looking over the investment before any decisions are made. This will increase the chances of picking up on the little details that can make or break a big deal. A strong co-op can also lead to more investments further down the road.

As with any business or investment opportunity, you also need to consult professionals to make sure all your bases are covered.

Conclusion

Due diligence is a positive process to learn as much as you can about a business or investment opportunity. Due diligence is essential to doing business successfully; it minimizes your risk and increases the likelihood of expected outcomes.

If you are making a decision with a significant amount of money at stake, then you want that decision to be as informed as possible. Whether you are making a transaction, partnering with an individual or company, or making an investment, it is important that you perform appropriate due diligence.

It is something that people on both sides of an opportunity need to do, but it also serves as an opportunity to develop relationships that are important for opportunity execution in the case of partnerships and investments.

Bio of Joseph Price

Joseph Price is CEO and Co-Founder of Triomphe Consulting. Joe brings over 10 years of experience in business development, market research, and management consulting for several industries, most notably the biotech, information technology, and renewable energy fields.

Early in his career, Joe worked with clients such as Sun Microsystems, IBM Global Services, Capgemini, and Hewlett Packard to identify and target new product and market opportunities - designing, testing, and executing market research and analysis methodologies for each client. During this time, he led a substantial number of engagements focused on understanding customer behaviors, mapping competitive landscapes, and validating growth strategies.

Following this work in IT and biotech, Joe joined the world of institutional investors and applied his analytical and critical mind to developing merger and acquisition strategy. This would include due diligence, market segmentation study, competitive landscape analysis, and financial modeling and valuation.

Joe has successfully led numerous projects to support strategic quantitative and qualitative analysis. Recently he has been very successful leading cross-border transaction focused initiatives, such as helping investors assess the strength of potential targets far from their shores.

Joe received his B.A. from Tufts University. In his spare time, he enjoys fishing with his niece and nephews, reading, and writing about his adventures.

http://www.triompheconsulting.com

6

Leveraging to Take Advantage of Opportunities

Many entrepreneurs will start out the GGD process by looking for opportunities and wading through all the technical aspects of the process. While these are obviously important steps, you cannot move forward adeptly unless you understand the assets you carry with you to go global. So, this is where we start.

As an entrepreneur, you likely do not have unlimited resources to allocate to going global, but at the same time you likely do not recognize all the resources that you have available to do so. This chapter is about opening your eyes to many different forms of resources that you can use to go global and using those strengths to build your opportunity and business model.

We will start off with a framework that will help you understand how to identify assets and strengths called the Leverage Point Strategy™.

The Leverage Point Strategy™ is a specific methodology based on the concept of leverage. Leverage is the ratio of change in input to the change in output. Greater leverage is gained when a small force multiplies output. The goal is to see a small force produce as much change in output as possible.

Leverage points are those forces, or points, that create the rate of change in output. The power of leverage points is on a continuum from low to high. The best scenario is to locate high leverage points, because, in these cases, the smallest amounts of force effect the greatest change or results.

A very clear analogy of how a leverage point works is the rudder of a ship. It is a small part of the ship in comparison with the size of the ship, but it creates a small force that is able to turn the ship in a new direction. In practical terms, maximizing leverage points makes use of small, but significant, forces.

Leverage points are related to tipping points. A tipping point is a point at which an object is displaced from one place to a new and different state. Leverage points are used to create the tipping point.

Malcolm Gladwell wrote the book *The Tipping Point: How Little Things Make a Big Difference.*[23] He identified three key factors, or types of leverage points, for creating tipping points: the Law of the Few, the Stickiness Factor, and the Power of Context.

The Law of the Few is when a few key types of people champion and catalyze an idea, or concept, to critical mass. The types of people are Connectors, Mavens, and Salesmen. When all three types of actors advocate an idea, the concept is more likely to reach a tipping point. Connectors, Mavens, and Salesmen are examples of leverage points. Each is a small force that can wield significant results.

The Stickiness Factor is something that sticks in the minds of individuals and influences their behavior in the future. And the Power of Context is when the right environment, or time, aligns with your business opportunity to create momentum.

Each of the leverage points highlighted by Gladwell can induce a tipping point, but it is more likely that the combination of these leverage points will actually force a tipping point.

Another category of leverage points is types of capital. In essence, these are the strengths you bring to the business opportunity overall. According to Dr. Bruce Cook of Kingdom Venture Capital, there are 13 types of capital:

- **Economic** includes currency, liquid assets, and finance.
- **Social** includes community-focused or socially responsible activities, such as relief work, charity, and scientific research.
- **Spiritual** refers to strength drawn from faith and your internal spirit.
- **Knowledge** is what you and your team know, both the intellectual and mental processes.

---

[23] Gladwell, M. (2002). *The Tipping Point: How Little Things Make a Big Difference*. New York, NY: Back Bay Books (Hatchette Book Group).

- **Political** refers to formal political affiliations and influence.
- **Environmental** refers to assets in the global "green" movement, like carbon credits.
- **Creative** includes your creativity, artistic expression, and intellectual property.
- **Positional** refers to the roles, titles, and authority you hold both formally and informally.
- **Institutional** includes formal reputation, influence, status, alliances, and partners.
- **Physical** refers to your body's capacity, including energy and fitness.
- **Generational** refers to legacy, heritage, family lineage, and wealth that are passed down in families.
- **Closeness** refers to the ability to draw close and also to be vulnerable, or open, in relationships.
- **Relational** refers to the span and depth of your relationships.

You may wonder how some types of capital (e.g., social) can serve as leverage points for business, but any form of capital can exert influence over business opportunities. For example, a young North American moved to Ghana and established a gold mine. His gold mine sits on land on which a local indigenous tribe lives. In addition to getting a mining concession from the government, he had to form an agreement with the local chief on how the operation would benefit the community beyond jobs. He agreed to build a school, among other things. In emerging markets, business is not separated from the complex system of society.

In actuality, many things are leverage points, including situations and circumstances. However, the leverage point might be in your favor or in someone else's, and the leverage point may have low or high impact. Your goal is to find a series of leverage points in your favor with high-impact potential.

The process of applying the Leverage Point Strategy™ works in conjunction with completing an environmental analysis, as well as a SWOT analysis, of your opportunities. Following these analyses, apply the Leverage Point Strategy™ by asking yourself the following questions:

- What are the key leverage points that will make an opportunity work?
- Which of the key leverage points have high, medium, or low impact?
- Which combinations of key leverage points will have the most impact?
- How will the key leverage points help to override the weaknesses and threats in an opportunity?
- In general, how will I incorporate the high-leverage points and high-leverage-point combinations into the business model?
- How will I know if the leverage points are working?

Once you have applied the Leverage Point Strategy™ to your analysis of opportunities, incorporate the leverage points into your business model appropriately. The business model gives a complete picture of how to implement the business successfully. It answers the question, "How do you logically create value?" Johan Wallin, in the book *Business Orchestration: Strategic Leadership in the Era of Digital Convergence,*[24] says a business model:

> ...defines the value-creation priorities of an actor (business) in respect to the utilization of both internal and external resources. It defines how the actor (business) relates with stakeholders, such as actual and potential customers, employees, unions, suppliers, competitors, and other internal groups. It takes account of situations where the actor's (business') activities may (a) affect the business environment and its own business in ways that create conflicting interests, or impose risks on the actor (business) or (b) develop new, previously unpredicted ways of creating value.

---

[24] Wallin, J. (2006). *Business Orchestration: Strategic Leadership in the Era of Digital Convergence.* New York, NY: Wiley.

In the book *Business Model Generation: A Handbook for Visionaries, Game Changers, and Challengers,*[25] Alexander Osterwalder and Yves Pigneur pose key questions to consider when developing a solid business model. The following is an adaptation focused on leverage points: "What key leverage points will you use to..."

- Activate your customer segments?
- Maximize your revenue streams?
- Improve offerings for your customer segments?
- Better relate to your customers over time?
- Maximize resource allocation to run the business?
- Improve efficiency and effectiveness of key activities in running the business?
- Better utilize and leverage the "people" assets used to run the business?
- Increase and improve outputs of key activities?
- Maximize partnerships, alliances, and collaboration?
- Maximize network and distribution channels to reach customers?
- Manage and reduce costs of running the business?

Leverage points are simply tangible and intangible assets, resources, situations, etc. that can be used to gain and sustain momentum in the business environment. As you analyze a business opportunity, or problem, identify leverage points. And, use leverage points to help you assess opportunities, as well as incorporate the best leverage points and combinations into the business model and operations.

There are numerous leverage points available to help build a going global strategy on top of your own strengths, but not necessarily tied to your partners. To get you started in the right direction, I will outline several common leverage points to explore in the following sections.

---

[25] Osterwalder, A., & Pigneur, Y. (2010). *Business Model Generation: A Handbook for Visionaries, Game Changers, and Challengers.* New York, NY: Wiley.

Demand-Driven Exporting

According to Lemak and Arunthanes[26], there are four types of international sales strategies: Domestic-Based Export Strategy, Domestic-Based Value-Added Strategy, Worldwide Value-Added Strategy, and Worldwide Volume Maximization Strategy. In the first two strategies, a firm's focus is on selling to the home market. International sales take only a small portion of a firm's total production, and the firm is therefore not dependent on international sales for sustainability. The difference between the first two strategies is that in the Domestic-Based Value-Added Strategy, more than 10% of a firm's production will occur outside the home country. In the last two international sales strategies, international sales account for more than 30% of a firm's success.

For small businesses and entrepreneurs, the first international sales strategy – Domestic Export-Based Strategy – is typically considered. Lemak and Arunthanes describe this strategy as one in which firms, "manufacture or assemble products in the home country to sell in the domestic market...(And) export a small portion of total production to foreign users with little or no modifications via distributors, agents, and/or their own sales subsidiaries." If a firm can find an international market with demand that allows it to sell its products with little or no modification, I would call this a leverage point with potentially high impact. This situation reduces the upfront cost to enter a new market by not having to adapt the product significantly.

Another important aspect to going global is to quickly operate in the black, say within six to 18 months. Small firms typically cannot absorb losses for any great length of time. So, it's important to find means to generate sales and cash more quickly.

---

[26] Lemak, D. & Arunthanes, W. (1997). Global Business Strategy: A Contingency Approach, *Multinational Business Review,* 5 (1), 26–37.

Finding markets with high demand and with limited supply is one way to accelerate operating in the black, particularly in emerging markets. *The Financial Times Lexicon* defines demand as, "the amount of a particular economic good or service that a consumer or group of consumers will want to purchase at a given price."

In emerging markets there is demand for many different things as consumers move up the socioeconomic scale. Even basic services like housing, water access and sanitation, and transport are lucrative markets. For example, housing markets in many African markets like Nigeria, Ghana, and Angola remained strong during the economic crisis. As a whole, construction grew over 12% in Nigeria for each of the last five years, including 2008 and 2009, when the economic crisis hit, according to the *African Statistical Yearbook 2010* by the African Development Bank (ADB).

There are also short-term demand opportunities, which global enterprises can use to catalyze a long-term strategy. Some businesses saw a golden opportunity to enter the South African market with the 2010 FIFA World Cup. The largest suppliers of the "vuvuzela" horn happened to be Chinese manufacturers like Ninghai Jiying Plastics Manufacturing Company, which exported the vuvuzelas to South Africa. While they barely generated a profit on the vuvuzelas, the Chinese companies can now grow into the South African market with other products that have longer-term demand.

Note: This same example illustrates a problem with export-only models that bring little value to local economies. By and large, local sentiment on the ground was that it was the "Chinese" FIFA World Cup as opposed to bringing more opportunities to locals. The undercurrent is not positive, and there is a major shift in what South Africans will allow to happen in major business platforms in the future. Global businesses need to look at ways to bring value to local economies as well as to themselves.

In demand-driven opportunities, your product or service should readily resonate with your market. If you have a product that is hard to sell, it will take longer to educate the market, reducing or eliminating the advantage you have with the demand-driven opportunity to accelerate sales and cash. Other considerations include how large the demand is and how long it will last.

And finally, you also need to remember the "price" aspect of the demand equation. Demand implies that there is a particular price at which high demand is driven. If your price is too high, you reduce the size of your market. And, if the price of the demand is too low for you to make a profit, it may not be the opportunity for you.

Consumer Demographics

As with any market opportunity, you need to understand your consumers. There are five cursory demographics with which to explore a going global strategy: population, urbanization, gender, age, and socioeconomic status.

The first demographic is the population of a particular country. The idea is to identify volume markets, or markets in which you will likely be able to make a profit or get a return on investment. Volume market considerations may depend on your type of business or sector. For example, a volume market for the Information and Communication Technologies (ICT) sector in Africa is a population greater than 10 million. According to the *World Factbook*, the following is a list of the top fifteen emerging and frontier markets by population in 2011:

1. China (1,336,718,015)
2. India (1,189,172,906)
3. Indonesia (245,613,043)
4. Brazil (203,429,773)
5. Pakistan (187,342,721)
6. Bangladesh (158,570,535)
7. Nigeria (155,215,573)
8. Russia (138,739,892)
9. Mexico (113,724,226)
10. Philippines (101,833,938)

11. Ethiopia (90,873,739)
12. Vietnam (90,549,390)
13. Egypt (82,079,636)
14. Turkey (78,785,548)
15. Democratic Republic of Congo (71,712,867)

Urbanization is another demographic consideration. It simply means the percentage of the population that lives in urban areas. For example, 77% of Mexico's people live in urban centers. Since that country has a population of over 100 million, that figure means that over 77 million people are in the urban markets of Mexico.

Urban areas are more concentrated and tend to have better transportation systems than rural areas in emerging markets. These factors can be critical for distributing to and reaching your market. The cost of supplying the market could be greatly reduced if there are few requirements for in-country transportation beyond the key entry point.

You may also want to consider the rate at which people are moving to urban centers in a country. In a country like Vietnam, with only 28% of its population of 89 million living in urban centers but an approximate 3% rate of urbanization per year, there will be more than 2.6 million new people living in urban centers each year.

Gender is another demographic consideration for your market. Men and women tend to have different spending and shopping patterns. Culture can also impact consumer patterns between men and women. For example, in some Muslim communities women and men are not allowed to mingle openly, so shops adjust for their customers and the culture.

Age tends to be more significant than gender. In many emerging markets, the number of people being born and the number of people under 40 are greater than in Western markets, like the U.S. or Germany. For example, more than 70% of Africa's population is currently 40 years old or younger.

Regions like Africa will continue to have high growth rates over the next generation. Africa's population is expected to reach over 2 billion in 2050, according to the United Nations Population Division. This will exceed the population of countries like China and India.

Finally, you need to consider what the socioeconomic status of your market is. While there is a large, growing middle class in emerging markets, consumers do not have the purchasing power of consumers in Western markets, which generally exceeds $30,000 per year per consumer. The annual purchasing power of a Chinese consumer was $7,600 (and $3,500 for an Indian consumer) in 2010, according to the *World Factbook.*.

Another socioeconomic indicator, which can be used to look at consumers in emerging markets, is the rate at which they are moving up the socioeconomic scale. If 10% of a population of 20 million moves up the socioeconomic scale to the next level in five years, this means 2 million will have more money to spend in the medium-term.

This indicator is also important because it is known that people's spending patterns change as they move up the socioeconomic scale. For example, people change their food consumption patterns to include more meat and dairy as they move up.

Language and Culture

Language is a critical consideration when looking where to do business globally. Imagine trying to get simple directions from someone who doesn't speak your language. Now apply that to doing business in a foreign country in another language. While the task is not impossible, you put yourself at a distinct disadvantage. Entering markets that speak the same language as you do is a leverage point in your favor. However, you must be aware of the different dialect and colloquial differences in the language as it is locally spoken. For example, a pick-up, or small truck, is called a "bakkie" in South Africa.

The top five most spoken languages in the world are Chinese (Mandarin, Cantonese, etc.), Spanish, English, Arabic, and Hindi, according to *Ethnologue.com.* For business communication, English and French are quite universal.

In emerging markets, some of the countries in which English is an official language include Hong Kong, Singapore, India, Philippines, Pakistan, and Sri Lanka, according to the *World Factbook.* In Africa over 20 countries, including Nigeria, Kenya, South Africa, Botswana, Tanzania, and Ghana, have English as an official language. In North America many Caribbean states/territories like Puerto Rico, U.S. Virgin Islands, Jamaica, and the Bahamas also have English as an official language.

You can also look at countries with multiple official languages; these may serve as a springboard into surrounding, non-English-speaking countries. How? In territories like Hong Kong, which is a part of China, people often speak multiple languages. If the people with whom you work in Hong Kong both speak a Chinese language and understand the culture of mainland China, they can possibly serve as intermediaries for you to access the large market on mainland China.

In Egypt, English is not official, but it is widely understood, and Arabic is an official language. Because of this, Egypt could be a springboard into the markets of the Middle East and North Africa (MENA), which have Arabic, but not English, as an official language. And Rwanda, located in East/Central Africa and in which both French and English are official languages, may provide linkages between French-speaking and English-speaking African nations.

For small enterprises entering non-English-speaking markets, the key criterion is to have competent and trustworthy people representing you and looking out for your interests. Typically, you will only be able to assess the quality of your associates as you work with them and develop the relationships. Another approach is to have a high-trust relationship with an English-speaking individual, or organization, who has strong, trusted partners that can be held accountable in the market of interest.

As you expand your interest in going global, you may consider language and culture immersion for key people in your organization over which you have more influence and who have your company's interest, as well as their own, at heart. For China, one resource to learn about its culture, arts, and language is the Confucius Institute, which has branches all over the world.

As mentioned before, determining whether you have trustworthy and competent associates is worth the effort to confirm because of the potential risk associated with not getting it right. In fact, this aspect is important to consider whether the market is English- or non-English-speaking.

However, the issue with trust may not only be whether a person is trustworthy, but also whether *you* have the ability to trust that person. Both aspects are important for building relationships necessary for going global.

Culture can be a significant factor in developing trust relationships with competent associates. Humans tend to trust people that are similar to themselves – those who have similar backgrounds, have similar socioeconomic status, or come from the same in-group. Professor Geert Hofstede said that, "culture is more often a source of conflict than synergy." A nation's culture can broadly be understood along five cultural dimensions, which according to Hofstede are:

- **Power distance** – the degree to which less powerful members of society find it acceptable or expect power to be unequal.
- **Individualism** – the degree to which a society is individualistic versus collectivistic.
- **Masculinity** – how roles are distributed between men and women in the society.
- **Uncertainty and avoidance** – the degree to which a society can deal with uncertainty and ambiguity.
- **Long-term orientation** – the degree to which a society has a long-term or short-term outlook.

While differences in culture tend to promote conflict rather than synergy, a savvy global entrepreneur will come to learn the differences and adapt to them to maximize opportunities. In fact, those differences may prove highly useful to you. For example, in Brazil the business culture embraces collaboration, an important facet of teamwork and building strong ecosystems. This is an asset you can use if you have Brazilian partners to strengthen your international business ecosystem.

Cities and Economic Hubs

In the early 1800s only 7% of the world's population lived in urban centers. Today over half of the world's population lives in urban centers. In 2050 about 70% of the world's population is expected to live in urban centers, according to the United Nations. The concentration of population into smaller areas offers entrepreneurs access to a larger market in a smaller geographic space.

Megacities are those with populations of more than 10 million. According to the *Principal Agglomerations of the World* by Thomas Brinkhoff, megacities in 2011 (and their populations) in emerging markets are:

1. Canton, China (25,400,000)
2. Shanghai, China (24,900,000)
3. Delhi, India (23,500,000)
4. Mumbai, India (23,200,000)
5. Mexico City, Mexico (22,000,000)
6. Sao Paolo, Brazil (21,000,000)
7. Manila, Philippines (20,400,000)
8. Jakarta, Indonesia (19,000,000)
9. Karachi, Pakistan (17,100,000)
10. Calcutta, India (16,400,000)
11. Beijing, China (16,100,000)
12. Moscow, Russia (16,100,000)
13. Cairo, Egypt (15,500,000)
14. Buenos Aires, Argentina (14,200,000)
15. Dhaka, Bangladesh (13,800,000)
16. Tehran, Iran (13,300,000)
17. Istanbul, Turkey (13,200,000)
18. Rio de Janeiro, Brazil (12,600,000)
19. Lagos, Nigeria (12,400,000)

Another variable to consider is the rate of urbanization. If the rate of urbanization is positive, it means the consumer markets will enlarge in cities. For example, Pakistan has a rate of urbanization close to 5%. Karachi, a city with a population over 17 million, will increase by at least 800,000 new people each year.

A challenge for many fast-growing cities is not having sufficient services – transport, housing, water, etc. Throughout history, even in places like New York City, informal settlements arose to take in new city dwellers. With these new settlements comes a strain on existing services, hitting both formal and informal settlements. This can cause problems for businesses that also need services. Power outages caused by overloading is one example.

However, this situation also creates unique opportunities for entrepreneurs who possess alternative means to provide services that the government cannot, such as clean water, energy, housing, and transport.

In addition to cities, economic hubs also offer tremendous opportunities. An economic hub is a concentrated area in and through which economic activity flows. If you identify a good hub, you can create new opportunities that flow to places with which the hub is connected.

In Africa, Nigeria serves as the major economic hub for West Africa. Egypt is the key economic hub for North Africa. Kenya serves as the key economic hub for East Africa. And South Africa is the major economic hub for Southern Africa.

South Africa generates about 20% of the economic activity for the entire African continent. Within South Africa, Gauteng Province is the economic hub for the country, with about 30% of economic activity centered there. Gauteng Province serves as a key economic hub not only for South Africa but also for the entire continent. In a news article published by the *Times* in South Africa, Mudunwazi Baloyi, General Manager of Investment, Trade and Projects Facilitation of the Gauteng Economic Development Agency (GEDA), said that Gauteng is the fourth-largest economy in Africa, after the countries of South Africa, Egypt, and Nigeria.

Both cities and economic hubs have another distinct advantage: they generally have more and better business services and supporting sectors. I like to call Sandton, a suburb of Johannesburg in Gauteng Province, the "Wall Street" or "Manhattan" of Africa. Inside the few square miles of Sandton's central business district is a great concentration of financial and economic activity, and multinational firms and visitors/representatives from almost every country can be found. Many of the largest and most significant business, political, and social conferences, workshops, and forums for the continent are held in Sandton.

In addition, Pretoria, Gauteng, has a large number of embassies and consulates, representing countries from all over the world. Generally, each country will have representatives that deal with commercial and economic interests housed in the embassy or consulate. So, from one economic hub a large number of regional and global business interests can be accessed.

Economic Zones and Clusters

Economic zones are geographic areas designated to promote trade and economic development within a country. They have more liberalized economic policies than the countries in which they reside, and these policies are highly conducive to both native and foreign business. Typical advantages for businesses and investors include tax incentives, better infrastructure, better institutions, better processes, and freer flow of international trade.

There are different forms of economic zones, from free ports to information-processing zones. Some economic zones around the globe include Hyderabad, New Delhi, and Pune in India; Subic and Bataan in the Philippines; and Dubna and Lipetsk in Russia.

China's growth story is very tied to the introduction of economic zones in the 1980s. For example, the Shenzhen Export Processing Zone was a small village and has now grown to almost the size of a megacity with around 9 million people. Not only are economic zones often better places to conduct business, but they may also offer the chance of a growing market.

Another model for concentrating and leveraging economic activity is clusters, most notably researched and introduced by Michael Porter. A cluster is a group of enterprises in close geographic proximity that produce similar or related products in a particular field – e.g., nanotechnology, leather, diamonds, etc. In Uganda, there are over 20 diverse clusters under development.

Globally, nations are seeing clusters as a means to spur economic development. For entrepreneurs, they may offer alliances, bringing expertise, value chains, and capacity, in a foreign country.

One of the models for economic clusters is Silicon Valley in San Jose, California. This technology cluster has created an ecosystem that drives technology innovation around the globe. Note that successful clusters also can spur connections with other markets and multinationals, such as the case with the automotive clusters in India. In the Chennai-Hosur-Bangalore region cluster, Toyota, Mitsubishi, Hyundai, and Ford are among the multinationals involved.

In essence, economic zones and clusters serve as pathways for entrepreneurs to enter new markets through the inherent strengths they bring. An enterprise can find expertise and ecosystems to support its singular effort to enter new markets while containing the strain on existing resources.

While country analysis is important for determining an opportunity for going global, taking a closer look at the strengths of specific economic zones or clusters within a country may help you discover leverage points in favor of doing business in that country even when the overall country analysis indicates that the business climate there is weak.

Trade and Investment Agreements

A trade agreement is one between two or more parties, possibly covering a wide range of tax, tariff, trade, and investment issues. In bilateral agreements between two countries like Canada and South Africa, there are preferential and protection measures that benefit businesses from both countries. Along with trade agreements, business councils are mandated by governments to represent the private sector. In some sense, they are similar to chambers of commerce.

Enterprises can incorporate the preferential and protection measures in trade agreements to leverage opportunities in a specific country. Typical concerns of those doing business overseas include the following: How easy is it to remove money from the host country? What protection is there for assets in the host country? These and other issues may be covered by trade or investment agreements.

Trade agreements also bring opportunities to network, since businesses generally form part of the diplomatic delegations accompanying government officials to discuss trade agreements. For example, President Jacob Zuma of South Africa took along over 350 businesspeople on his state visit to China in 2010. This offers businesses unique access to people and organizations in the host country.

Also, business councils serve as excellent channels to gain information, contacts, and expertise on operating in a foreign country. In a recent example, I had a person approach me who needed very specific information about getting a product through customs in Algeria. I contacted the U.S.–Algeria Business Council, and they were readily able to identify the organization that could assist. For someone trying to retrieve this information on his or her own, the process could have taken several weeks.

As mentioned in an earlier chapter, check with your foreign affairs office to find out what trade agreements are in place.

Regional Economic Communities

Like economic hubs, regional economic communities (RECs) can provide a strategic focus for businesses and investors. RECs focus on creating at least a free trade area, customs union, and common market between member countries. While this helps the member countries with cross-border trade and opens markets to the world, it also provides larger and more varied opportunities for businesses and investors.

The European Union (EU) is a prime example. The *World Factbook* says the population of the EU is around 500 million in 2011, compared with about 85 million in Germany, its most populated member state. The purchasing power of 500 million people is obviously greater than that of 85 million.

The goal of an REC is to make the movement of factors of production, as well as goods and services, between member countries as easy as within the countries. This will guarantee efficient resource use, which is a competitiveness factor that can attract investment and boost economic growth. For entrepreneurs, it means that a free trade agreement in the REC will allow your products to move from one country to another with few or no tariffs and make it easier for you to reach across borders within the region to expand your market.

As an example, if you planned to concentrate your business and investment ventures in the East Africa economic hub of Kenya, you would greatly benefit from the ICT infrastructure and institutions developed for the East Africa Community (EAC). The EAC consists of Burundi, Kenya, Rwanda, Tanzania, and Uganda. It has a combined population of about 140 million, compared with about 40 million in Kenya alone. For those who do business and invest in consumer markets, the difference in market potential based on size is significant.

RECs can also help businesses more successfully navigate within many countries simultaneously by harmonizing policies, incentives, etc., between member states. For example, the EAC is working on a regional investment code, which means foreign businesses and investors will have one code with which to engage, as opposed to five.

Detractors of the U.S. experience with the North American Free Trade Agreement (NAFTA) have claimed that it has served as a means for jobs to be exported so that companies could pay less for labor. However, services or products that can be reproduced elsewhere by someone else with cheaper labor will not help sustain your business or even national economies, because these services or products have a high probability of being substituted.

The key for entrepreneurs is to develop competitive products and services with a low likelihood of substitution. This can lead to more jobs in your home country and the foreign markets you enter.

Innovation is key to sustainability. If your company is not innovative, going global will not solve your long-term sustainability issues.

Conclusion

Creating leverage and knowing when and how to use it effectively is critical for a small business to be able to make big moves. There are several common leverage points that you can consider when looking at markets and business environments. One common leverage point is consumer demographics. Others include language and culture, economic zones and clusters, trade and investment agreements, and regional economic communities.

Identifying and acting upon leverage points are key in your strategy formulation and execution processes for going global. Leverage points become embedded in your business model, as well as in business operations. They help you keep your strategy dynamic.

7

Powering Your Own Going Global Network

Being a global organization is not just a mantra for tapping marketplaces around the world. It is, in fact, a new paradigm shift – a new reality. For today's companies, global is not something they do but something they are.

"Born Global" firms, a term coined by McKinsey and Associates, are those that provide products or services globally from birth. According to research by McKinsey, Born Global firms see the world as their marketplace from the beginning, not as an expansion to their domestic markets. These firms will often implement their global strategy within two years from inception.

In fact, more firms than ever go global right from the start each year. Neal Gandhi, author of "Born Global" and CEO of Quick Start Global, says this is part of our business future. Gandhi says that Born Global firms are efficient. By efficient, he means use of resources is optimized. Firms place their legal headquarters, teams of talent, and capital around the globe where it makes the most sense. That means a company's legal headquarters could be in Mauritius, its development team in India, its artistic team in the United States, and sales and marketing teams spread across the globe.

These may sound like multinational firms, but they aren't. These firms often employ less than 25 people in their first few years. Another term for these firms is micro-multinationals.

Born Global firms do differ from traditional multinationals in that they do not consider borders per se in their strategy. Gandhi indicates that since regulations like taxation vary from country to country and the concept of borders are still very strong as to how governments regulate business, the environment for business for a Born Global is quite complex without the resources of a multinational to address it. But Gandhi points out that a Born Global entrepreneur takes challenges like this in stride.

Gandhi says the one key factor for a Born Global firm is the right people. Born Global firms need people that are passionate, trustworthy, buy into the vision, and can execute in the local context.

A Born Global Firm in Action

Ashifi Gogo is CEO of Sproxil, Inc., a Born Global firm operationalized first in Africa. Gogo indicates that Sproxil's global strategy was a natural result of the challenge Sproxil was designed to address - counterfeit products.

Sproxil's initial product to eliminate counterfeit drugs has a global value chain. Many legitimate brand and generic pharmaceuticals are manufactured in India and China, and then sold in Africa. So, its customer base spans several countries and, therefore, it does as well.

Gogo says that ICT, mobile phones, and broadband have made a significant difference in managing costs, work, and reducing the number of visits to Africa. The Sproxil team is able to stay connected regularly with each other and clients in Africa by VOIP and video calls.

Sproxil's team is spread across the Atlantic – in the United States and Africa. When asked for a photo of the entire team, Gogo couldn't produce one as the entire team had never met in one location.

So, technology has served as a key enabler for Sproxil to operate globally. However, Gogo says it is important to also find trusted local partners who can work well remotely using ICT and understand the markets you are entering.

Addressing Challenges of Forming a Global Venture

Global firms have the same challenges as local or regional firms. They need the right people, right resources, right information, and right capital to tap business opportunities. However, finding the right combination of these for a successful business strategy is more complex. As soon as you look to do cross border engagement of any type, you immediately add complexity which can seem insurmountable.

However, the key to any successful Born Global venture as noted by Gandhi and Gogo is people. In this connected world, you are only a few steps away from people who can help you find the right people, right resources, right information, and right capital. The right people do not need to be in your organization. You just need access to them to get to everything else.

You see, people are the owners, stewards, and gatekeepers to what you need. What you don't have, someone else can provide. That's why I say that going global is not only a matter of what you have, but also what you can tap into.

At the heart of every successful firm today, is a network, or ecosystem, which is both internal and external to the organization. If you can build this network to provide the necessary support for your global venture, you will be well ahead of others when implementing global opportunities.

In essence, your goal is to become the network facilitator of an ecosystem that will support your business venture. You will not own the majority of resources and assets needed for your business venture, but you will be able to marshal what's needed through your ecosystem.

James Moore, in *Predators and Prey: A New Ecology of Competition*,[27] described an ecosystem for economic pursuits as:

> *An economic community supported by a foundation of interacting organizations and individuals--the organisms of the business world. This economic community produces goods and services of value to customers, who are themselves members of the ecosystem. The member organizations also include suppliers, lead producers, competitors, and other stakeholders...*
>
> *...Over time, they co-evolve their capabilities and roles, and tend to align themselves with the directions set by one or more central companies. Those companies holding leadership roles may change over time, but the function of ecosystem leader is valued by the community because it enables members to move toward shared visions to align their investments and to find mutually supportive roles.*

---

[27] Moore, J. (1993). Predators and Prey: A New Ecology of Competition, *Harvard Business Review*, May/June.

As the network facilitator, you are seen to provide key value which then opens the door for you to access other people, resources, information, capital, etc. for your business purpose. Companies like IBM, Apple, etc. are doing this successfully, but you don't need to be big to serve in this role. You can apply the same principles to small networks.

The role of network facilitator is well-suited for global business as today's global businesses place elements of their value chain where it makes the most sense. Network facilitators connect people and build networks where it makes sense.

One simple example is based on advice from Dennis Hessler of Spyglass Point Productions, who helps people start small exporting businesses. Choose an industry, or product, that you understand and would be considered an expert. Find a local manufacturing firm that does little or no exporting and offer to serve as its liaison to developing markets overseas. Then, work on locating foreign buyers. However, where you add value is in managing the entire process for the firm not just in making sales. If you create value, the firm will not want to work around you or will find it difficult to do so.

While you have started with one firm, you have developed a small ecosystem to support this client, including export and import research, market research, freight forwarders and customs experts, etc. You can use this same ecosystem to support other clients and as the ecosystem expands you can look at spin-off opportunities.

A key imperative you need to follow in order to be successful in developing powerful networks and ecosystems is creating value for people and organizations.

Building a Dynamic Network

I, myself, am a task-oriented person. This means I travelled the hard road to learn the significance of people in getting results and business success. My training ground was Africa for close to eight years now. While expertise plays a part in my success, relationships also play a significant role.

When I started to research the notion of social networks, I learned that social networking was even important for Bill Gates. When Gates started his firm, his mother used her social connections in Seattle to provide Gates access to key business people.

One of my biggest observations is that social networks are very important when one is initiating a new idea, whether in business or covering social issues. So, just as we spend time developing the next great idea, we need to focus on developing the ecosystem that will support the idea through its lifecycle.

A network is an interconnected system of things or people. Social networks are human networks we belong to, defined by relationships.

However, social networks in their raw form are not leveraged for business. In order to produce a strong network that will lead to business results, it has to have a purpose. So, to tap the power of our networks we need to transform them from social to value (purpose driven) networks. Value networks consist of people who come together in a loose association to achieve some economic, political, or social good.

Pay special attention to two phrases – "value" and "loose association." First, our whole business and economic systems are based on value creation. People, and organizations made up of people, have the ability to take raw materials and transform them into something of value for others, including things for which people will exchange something of value, e.g., money, knowledge, land, resources.

A value chain is the series of value-added activities involved to deliver valuable products and services to the end consumer. For example, a farmer grows string beans which he harvests and sells to an agricultural processor like Del Monte. Del Monte cooks and cans the string beans, then transports the product to wholesalers and distributors. The wholesalers and distributors will finally get the product to stores where people can purchase them. In today's application of value chains, many firms refer to their supply chains and distribution channels as their value chains which can make creating value just seem like a technical exercise.

It is attitudes like this which have divorced value from business. Financial institutions create complex instruments from which they can make money, but don't represent value. Day traders cause volatility in stock markets because they make their money from finding gaps in the market not value. It's hard to tell what value is really in the stock market today. And at some point, these attitudes and behaviors cave in on themselves, skewing markets and business.

If we take a closer look at a value network, we find that our network of people represent value because they own, have access to, or have stewardship over information, resources, capital, etc. So, we want to be able to identify the value held within it and leverage it to shape our business strategies.

And in this perspective of business, it is the strengths in these loose associations in the value network, as well as your own strengths, that determine the opportunities of which you are able to take advantage. Therefore, when I say that you can "go global on a dime" it means that every resource, asset, knowledge, and bit of cash you put in it goes further because you work with others that bring what they can to the table, allowing all of you to go further.

Network Weaving

The process to build this network, or ecosystem, is based on principles but moves dynamically. Networks, because they involve people, are fluid, dynamic, and constantly changing, so our approaches must match.

Healthy networks are like grapevines, which produce fruit. As they are cultivated, the grapevines produce new fruit every harvest – they multiple.

Healthy networks should also multiply. When they do, your access to resources, information, capital, influence, etc. grows. And just like grapevines, they need to be cultivated to yield good fruit. Cultivating can involve pruning back some relationships, cutting some relationships, grafting some relationships together, and watering some relationships.

In cultivating a network, you have an active role not a passive one. Valdis Krebs, and others, has coined the phrase, "network weaver," for this role.[28] A network weaver takes responsibility for building healthy networks.

Network weavers look like people we call "social butterflies," but they network, or cross-pollinate ideas, resources, and opportunities for people with a purpose. Social butterflies network just to network.

Network weavers also watch, weave, and wake up networks in order to create value for people. They operate out of the heart (spirit) first, then the head (mind) and hands (body). They innately see the value of people and want to provide value to people.

There are three principles for successful network weavers whether it is for business, political, or social good. First, they love what they do and love people.

Second, they serve, share with, and sacrifice for people. It is not about "I," but about "we."

Third, they create win-win situations for stakeholders, not just shareholders. The goals are to do no harm and no one needs to lose. We see the opposite of this in public companies on the stock market where there is push to increase the stock price and dividends to shareholders while communities, employees, and others are harmed by the extreme nature of pursuing stock prices and dividends.

This principle is very important in emerging markets where even though there are huge opportunities, most of the countries have huge development challenges like poverty, poor health, and poor education. It is not ethical to only look at how you can make money and not consider how to support the local economies. It can be as simple as working with a local partner who employs people. By working with that local company, you are supporting the local economy. In fact, you will learn later that this is one key method for you to manage and reduce risks and costs.

---

[28] Krebs, V. & Holley, J. Building Smart Communities through Network Weaving. Accessed online at http://www.orgnet.com/BuildingNetworks.pdf.

There are seven major activities involved with network weaving:

- **Meet and greet** – Network and be open to meeting new people anywhere, anytime. Introduce others.
- **Manage** – Stay in touch with people. Seek them out to see how they are doing and what they are doing.
- **Mention** – Seed something useful to your network.
- **Map** – Know the people, relationships, and activities of your network.
- **Mesh** – Bring people together around a purpose or common interest (Tribes).
- **Mobilize** – Assist the network to organize around purpose or common interest.
- **Move** – Get the network to act.

The first four activities deal more with one-on-one interactions while "Mesh," "Mobilize," and "Move" deal more with developing the network you need to support your business venture.

The "Meet and Greet" activity involves making new connections and connecting people. When you meet a new person, you want to listen and learn from them. You can ask yourself the following questions and take mental notes:

- Who is s/he?
- What is his/her passion, purpose, or interests?
- What are his/her strengths?
- Why is s/he here?
- Is there an opportunity to help him/her?

When you connect people, you are "leading them to the water." You are leading them to people with which you believe they can form a mutual relationship. In the process, you want to consider the following questions and take mental notes:

- Who they are?
- How do you know or how did you meet them?
- What are their common passions, purposes, or interests?
- How might they be able to help each other?

When actually making the connection between people, Jack Ricchiuto of *Designinglife.com* says there are different levels of introduction which involve varying levels of your involvement. For example, you recently met Tom and believe that there would be mutual benefit if he met Shakira, who has a common interest and complementary capacities. You have the option to introduce them in the following ways:[29]

1. Suggest Tom should speak to Shakira.
2. Suggest Tom should speak with Shakira and call Shakira to look for a contact.
3. Introduce Tom to Shakira in an email.
4. Introduce Tom to Shakira in a conference call.
5. Introduce Tom to Shakira in person.
6. Introduce Tom and Shakira in person and follow up with them to nurture connection.
7. Introduce Tom and Shakira and offer a collaboration opportunity to get Tom and Shakira off to a successful partnership.

Levels 6 and 7 are both meaningful and most productive, if you feel led to use these approaches. As your network grows, you will not be able to offer this level of interaction for everyone, but you can still connect them effectively to help nurture their networks and yours.

The "Manage" and "Mention" activities are those you conduct after you have met people. Manage involves three key elements:

*   Make note of the person right after you meet them. Your notes should include name, contact information, passion/purpose/ interest, strengths, and anything else you can remember of interest. Personal details about family and likes and dislikes will often help open conversations.
*   Follow up in a timely manner. Acknowledge that it was nice to meet the person, and complete anything you promised.
*   Keep in contact periodically.

The "Mention" activity is simply connecting people that you know with people, resources, or information they will find beneficial. This means that as you meet new people or come across new information, think about who

---

[29] Ibid.

would find this new opportunity beneficial or valuable. Don't get into the habit of sending out mass mailings, which do not reflect the personal touch of sharing something you think will be beneficial.

The "Manage" and "Mention" activities should be done with some regularity as it allows you to reach out to people that you may not see often. Checking in once a year is a good general policy, by phone, if possible. You never know what someone has been up to and what new collaborations are possible as things have likely changed in both his/her business and yours. As you will learn later, having the right people working with you can cut cost, time, and risk, so setting aside time to reach out to others is an investment that can pay off big.

The best tools for managing the "Manage" and "Mention" activities are still contact management or email programs with calendar and task features. Many of the social tools like Facebook, Linkedin, Twitter, and MySpace are nice connection platforms and can augment what you do; however, they do not help you manage information, tasks, or resources well. Many email programs now, like Outlook, allow you to integrate your social network accounts into your inbox.

You will learn how to tap the advantage of trust to complete the remaining three activities in network weaving – Mesh, Mobilize, and Move – in the next chapter *Leveraging Trust Networks*.

The Importance of "Personal Touch" in Building Networks

Most people I share with on how to build their networks tell me they have never thought of managing their connections this way. They go to events and collect cards that sit on a desk somewhere. I remind them that they are missing opportunities. Meeting someone is a value encounter that you do not want to waste.

The best example in my own experience was the work I did with youth entrepreneurs in South Africa. There always seemed to be some bump in the road because people didn't see the value of having youth entrepreneurs in a business ecosystem. At the time, I was working on for-profit business models that would also lead to inclusive opportunities for young entrepreneurs that didn't have much business experience but could learn and provide service with the right opportunities.

I would frequently get comments like, "Why are you working with young people? They cannot offer you anything." But what many people failed to realize is that those young people understood their local communities and often had contact with important figures because of tribal affiliations. Now, I have access to the very markets everyone else is trying to tap. I looked for value where others didn't see any. This can be part of your success as well.

I hope you will approach network weaving as a means to identify the value everyone can bring and the value you can bring to others. When you are able to identify value and then shape business strategy around the unique value that your stakeholders bring to the table, you will be able to anticipate and execute where others fail. And while it does take an investment of your time and energy, once your value network is sufficiently established it will help you tap opportunities faster and with less cost and risk overall.

The process of network weaving also promotes the creation of goodwill, a social currency. The *Merriam-Webster Dictionary*[30] defines goodwill as, "a kindly feeling of approval and support," "benevolent interest or concern," or "the favor or advantage that a business has acquired especially through its brands and its good reputation." In fact, goodwill is an intangible asset that is included in accounting practices. It is the value that a company has beyond its book value. Marshall Fields said, "Goodwill is the only asset that competition cannot undersell or destroy."

When someone has goodwill toward you, he or she will more likely share his or her knowledge, assets, and connections with you. Creating goodwill leads to influence. Goodwill is also a type of trust. As mentioned before, trust can be used as the basis to create a network in which to launch successful going global ventures.

---

[30] http://www.m-w.org

Conclusion

If you didn't fully understand how important networks can be before reading this chapter, then hopefully you do now. By honing your networking skills you can acquire connections that stretch around the globe and back.

Aim to be a network weaver and introduce people to each other as they have done for you. Your networks should be ever expanding and along with it your access to resources, information, capital, influence, etc. will grow. Once you develop your networks, you need to use the value held within them to shape your business strategies.

8

Leveraging Trust Networks

On any day, you will find people exchanging things of value. A typical example is a person buying a product from a vendor with cash or credit. However, value can be exchanged in a variety of ways including exchanges of information, services, resources, and products. Exchanges happen between individuals, businesses, organizations, and governments at inconceivable rates of speed, particularly with the advent of electronic payment systems and the Internet.

While the idea of exchanging value may be a simple concept, it is played out in a complex environment. For example, the value chain to deliver cars to customers involves an entire ecosystem of agents, people, and organizations. There are the designers and engineers that draw the blueprint for the car. There are firms that transform raw materials into parts. There are other firms that take parts and transform them into components. Then, there are firms that assemble the vehicles. And consider the transport, distribution, and sales systems which support the entire value chain.

One common denominator in all forms of value exchange is trust. Both sides of the exchange trust they are getting the value expected from the exchange, trusting each other to provide the value expected or agreed upon. According to the *Merriam-Webster Dictionary*[31], trust is the, "assured reliance on the character, ability, strength, or truth of someone or something."

---

[31] Ibid.

Kenneth Arrow, an international economist, said as economic and social interactions become more complex, trust becomes the lubricant to keep things moving.[32] Oil lubricates engine parts to reduce friction between moving parts while improving efficiency and reducing wear; trust acts in a similar way for business transactions, markets, and economic systems.

Anthony Giddens said that as societal and organizational processes modernize trust also becomes more important.[33] Georg Simmel suggests that individual and collective wealth would not exist today without trust.[34]

If trust is so important to economic interaction, can it be used to leverage global business opportunities? And if so, how can it be used?

In fact, trust is already leveraged to take advantage of global business opportunities. The example that affects all of us is "fiat" money. Fiat money, which is typically thought of as paper but also includes coins, is currency which a government decrees is legal tender. Fiat money has no intrinsic value but we trust the government issuing the currency is backed by something of value.

We can look to the example of Zimbabwe to see what happens when fiat money is not backed by something of value and a government is not trusted to deliver something of value against it. Zimbabwe experienced hyperinflation in the latter half of the first decade of the 21st century. The Zimbabwean government continued to print more bank notes without any evidence they were backed by something of value. At one point in 2009, the government planned to issue different denominations of (e.g. 10, 50) trillion Zimbabwean dollar notes, which would have been valued well below $100.

More and more businesses and people began to use foreign currency, refusing to accept Zimbabwe's local currency. People even exchanged mobile phone minute scratch cards as a form of currency. They no longer

[32] Arrow, K. (1974). *Limits of Organization*. New York: W.W. Norton & Company.
[33] Giddens, A. (1990). *The Consequences of Modernity*. Stanford, CA: Stanford University Press.
[34] Simmel, G. (1978). *The Philosophy of Money*. London: Routledge & Kegan Paul.

trusted in Zimbabwe's legal tender. In the end, Zimbabwe stopped circulation of its local currency and the U.S. Dollar and South African Rand became the country's legal tender, along (theoretically) with the Euro and the British Pound.

This example illustrates trust at work in major systems, but there are many practical examples in everyday business. A manager who delegates tasks to subordinates, but then micromanages them, does not trust them. Micromanagement leads to de-motivation and bad team dynamics, which will ultimately cost.

There are other ways that trust can be leveraged to do global business. Research has shown that trust improves negotiations, increases flow of information, increases ability to learn, increases flexibility in management, increases speed of business transactions, and reduces costs, such as costs of transaction, governing relationships, agency, and opportunity.[35]

Trust is actually a strategic resource, according to Jay Barney and Mark Hansen, and can lead to competitive advantage when strong trust exists.[36] But more than a resource that can be used up and depleted, it is a strategic asset that if developed and managed correctly will only grow.

Imagine being a firm whose partners and customers always come back for more, are loyal, and help build business by word of mouth. In this scenario, both your tangible and intangible assets rise. This can create a unique niche for you in the market. Apple has consistently delivered to its customers, so they keep coming for more.

Unfortunately, trust is seen as being intangible by most, leading to the perception that building it, managing it, and leveraging it is a shot in the dark. However, according to Steven Covey in the *Speed of Trust*[37], this is

---

[35] Bachmann, R., & Zaheer, A. (eds.) (2006). *Handbook of Trust Research.* Cheltenham, UK: Edward Elgar Publishing
[36] Barney, J.B., & Hansen, M.H. (1994). Trustworthiness as a Source of Competitive Advantage. *Strategic Management Journal, 15*, 175-190.
[37] Covey, M.R. (2008). *The Speed of Trust: The One Thing that Changes Everything.* New York, NY: Free Press (Simon & Schuster).

far from the truth. Covey says that there are 13 behaviors of high-trust leaders, including showing loyalty, talking straight, creating transparency, and delivering results.

To manage the "how" of leveraging trust in business, there must be a sufficient framework to apply. Covey presents different spheres of trust as the "Five Waves of Trust." The first wave (Self-Trust) is to trust yourself. The second wave (Relationship Trust) is trust others.

The third through fifth waves represent "systems" of trust, including organizational, market, and societal. Covey refers to these "systems" of trust as Stakeholder Trust. Organizational Trust (the third wave) focuses on internal stakeholders while Market and Societal Trust (the fourth and fifth waves) focus on external stakeholders.

Covey's concept of Stakeholder Trust is on target, but it bypasses the dynamic, fluid, and complex nature of these systems. Covey's perspective does not adequately address inter-organizational/inter-market systems like joint ventures, alliances, partnerships, and value chains, which dominate the business environment today. Yet, trust is the vital center for coordinating interaction in such systems, according to Bill McEvily, Vincenzo Perrone, and Akbar Zabeer.[38]

Another perspective, which accounts for the dynamic, fluid, and complex nature of stakeholder systems, is thinking of them as networks. A simple definition of a network is an interconnected system of things or people.

Networks are composed of nodes and their relationships. In people networks like markets, the nodes are people. The key questions for these networks are: 1) Who are the people?, 2) How do they relate?, and 3) What do these relationships exchange and produce?

The concept of networks frames the business context in which trust plays a key role. Networks can frame organizations, industries, value chains, and markets. These are systems designed to create or increase value to its stakeholders. So when we speak of business or economic systems, we

---

[38] McEvily, B., Perrone, V., & Zabeer, A. (2003). Trust as an organizing principle. *Organization Science, 14*(1), 91-103.

are speaking of "value" networks. "Value networks are any web of relationship that generates both intangible and tangible value through complex, dynamic exchanges between two or more individuals, groups, or organizations," according to Verna Allee of Value Networks.[39] This describes the networks that surround business and economic systems to a tee.

In actuality, trust and value brought by agents to an exchange both impact the exchange, but there aren't clear, precise boundaries for how these two elements interact, influence each other, and impact exchanges. For business, it's enough to know that trust can be leveraged for global business and that there are practical, simple ways to do so within the context of what I call "trust" networks.

A trust network is an overlay for a value network. The degree and type of trust that exists between people is one factor in determining what value they are willing to exchange and how they view and work in the relationship. So, as mentioned previously, trust has the central vital role for coordinating economic and value interactions and exchanges. Simply put, use trust to guide, organize, and manage your global business opportunities.

The concept of a trust network is not entirely new. On the web, in a similar fashion, trust networks exist. They are used so people can declare who they trust so others can see. There are other similar networks like reputation, which are normal for marketplaces and payment systems like Amazon, eBay, and PayPal. Users that have more people who trust them, or uphold their reputations, tend to draw business their way.

The power of trust networks is that anyone can put them to use for business. You don't need a certain amount of money, connections (a lot of people have connections that do not have high trust), information, and resources. As you work the methodology of trust networks, these things naturally come as you build the right flows to achieve business success.

---

[39] http://www.vernaallee.com

Steps for Building a Trust Network for Global Business

One of the key misperceptions of going global is that you have to grow into it, developing enough capital resources to take on foreign markets. In reality, with the advent of telecommunications, the Internet, and technology, the cost of doing business globally can be a lot lower and within the budget and capacity of entrepreneurs and SMEs. Today, the resources into which you can tap, along with your own assets, shape your business opportunities. Hence, the importance of networks, particularly those built on trust, is evident because they allow you to tap into additional resources you do not have on your own.

Going global for an entrepreneur, or SME, can be costly, risky, and time consuming if done on his or her own. However, when you bring trusted associates into the equation, they can help spread the risk and reduce the time and cost to market.

Trust networks for global business start with the social and business networks an individual already has. An individual or organization works with "trusted" associates, configuring business strategy around the trust relationships and the information, resources, people, and capital they bring along with them.

The first step is to identify people within your formal, or informal, social and business networks who you trust. These are individual trust relationships. Openly talk about your business interests. It is often in these dialogues that opportunities appear.

The second step is to "chain" the individual trust relationships into a single, or a few, business opportunities. This results in a trust value chain to implement a business venture. If you choose the right trust relationships and opportunity frame, you can use this same chain over and over again to provide additional products and services to the same target market. The image on the next page illustrates a trust value chain spanning the United States (U.S.), Nigeria (NG), and South Africa (RSA) and the key roles played by the actors.

Value Chain

Phase 1

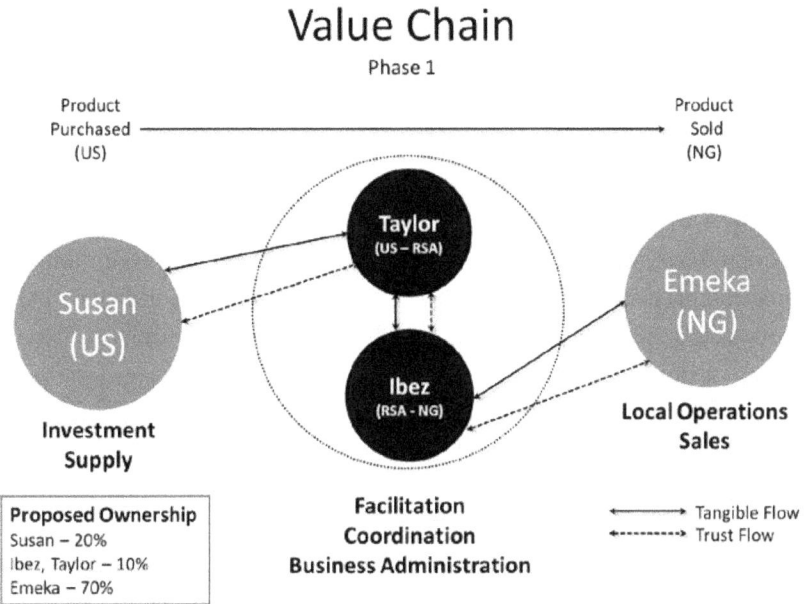

Product Purchased (US) ————————————→ Product Sold (NG)

Taylor (US – RSA)

Susan (US)

Emeka (NG)

Ibez (RSA - NG)

Investment Supply

Local Operations Sales

| Proposed Ownership |
| Susan – 20% |
| Ibez, Taylor – 10% |
| Emeka – 70% |

Facilitation
Coordination
Business Administration

————→ Tangible Flow
◄-------→ Trust Flow

In dealing with any global business opportunity, it is recommended to work with people you trust locally. You cannot micromanage, nor should you, from a distance. So, trust value chains are one method for conducting business. This method allows quick and effective action with business opportunities.

For example, we recently identified a product in the United States that would be highly useful in Africa. Because we are familiar with the local markets, we have identified several sectors and consumers that would readily use the quality product. We didn't spend a lot of time in feasibility because we could enter the market for little cost and allow it to grow. However, to make it work, we identified a small investor and supplier from the U.S. to manage purchasing the product and someone locally in Africa to sell it. These were identified and established through individual relationships.

In another example, we used trust to improve the effectiveness of a project. In a recent experience, we re-configured a new venture by placing a point of contact between two key stakeholders that both of them trusted.

And the third step is to repeat steps 1 and 2 to establish a trust network, which multiplies the economic opportunities and growth for everyone involved. In the dynamics of networks, healthy networks will become alive and grow on their own. But you have to start with strategic intent, not a haphazard approach.

Trust is a Strategic Asset

As mentioned earlier, trust is also a strategic asset. It's important to view your trust network not only as a vehicle to do business globally, but more so as assets that can grow and increase in value themselves if managed well. Not doing so is probably the primary downfall of any trust network. Individuals in the network begin to take the people and relationships for granted and stop putting in the proper care to make sure the network remains healthy.

It's important to realize what it means for someone to trust you. That person is willing to become vulnerable to you with the expectation that you will not harm him or her through intention or behavior. In business, that person or organization is expecting you to look out for his or her interest as well as your own.

The trust relationship established with someone is not the only sphere to consider when managing a trust network. You also need to acknowledge the impact and influence created on spheres within business, community, and society.

Individual trust relationships directly impact and influence organizations to which those in the trust relationship belong. For example, the information exchange between two people in different organizations, as a part of a joint venture, can help both organizations become more competitive in the market. On the other hand, a consultant (advising a technology company), who learns the details of a new technology roll-out, and shares these details with outsiders so they can buy or sell stock in anticipation of this move, violates the trust the technology company placed in the consultant.

This last example has broader implications because it gives the stock traders an unfair advantage over others, who might choose to buy or sell the stock. And, this type of breach of trust is actually against the law. The consultant has bankrupted his trust asset base just in this one act.

So, as you manage your portfolio of assets to grow wealth, you do the same with trust assets.

Building Trust in Individual Relationships

Since individuals are the lowest common denominator in a trust network, they should be seen as the essential building blocks for a trust network. As an individual, you need to consider both how you trust yourself and how you trust others. Healthy high-trust relationships can only be developed when individuals are able to trust themselves and willing to trust others. When considering your position in trust relationships, you should ask and address the following questions:

- Do you trust yourself to operate with integrity?
- Do you trust yourself to bear good intentions to others who trust you?
- Do you trust that you have the capacity to carry out what is asked of you? Within which boundaries, do you trust your capacity?
- Do you trust yourself to get results?
- Are you more prone to trust or distrust others?

Individuals inherently trust themselves and others in some instances and distrust in other instances. A few ways to engender trust within yourself:

- Learn to operate within the strengths and value you bring. Keep from being drawn into situations where you know you can't deliver.
- Only promise what you feel comfortable delivering.
- Deliver more than you promise.
- Don't be too critical of yourself. Be willing to forgive your own faults.

To engender trust within individual trust relationships, do the following:

- Listen more and when you do speak, speak plainly and straightforward.
- Show respect and deference for others.
- Be transparent as appropriate.
- Make yourself accountable to others and hold others accountable.
- Clarify expectations and keep commitments.
- Work on making relationships better.
- Be loyal.
- Correct mistakes or wrongdoings.
- Be alert for conflicts of interest and make others aware when they exist.
- Become vulnerable to the other person in the trust relationship.
- Share or give something to the other person in the trust relationship that they would value without asking for anything back.
- Keep someone's secrets whether or not they ask you to.
- If you make a mistake, whether you are caught or not, confess at the appropriate time and venue and ask for forgiveness.
- Be willing to lay down your interests for the interests of others when called for.

Applying Trust in Business Scenarios

In business, people tend to mostly think of the value others bring when entering agreements. That is the first decision point, but the second decision point, and often the final decision point, should be do you trust the person?

If you have any qualms on trusting the person at any level, you need to configure the agreement so that you are comfortable with the level of trust you are placing in the person. For example, a person has performed well for others previously, but your project has a much larger scale. If possible, split the project between two people if you cannot find one person with which you feel comfortable.

There are other times when you have to stretch your "trust" muscles to take advantage of opportunities. Find ways to minimize risks within these trust relationships. For example, configure project or venture so that breach of trust brings big negative consequences. If a person is looking to grow his or her business within a certain network or market in which you have a lot of influence, shape agreement so the individual understands the power your relationship brings and the loss he or she would experience if things didn't work out.

If you cannot establish a level of trust that will work for the project or venture, think about walking away for the time being. Often, people who enter agreements in these instances look for problems and micromanage others, which puts undue stress on the relationship and adds intangible and tangible costs to the project.

When considering entering, the current state of, or future of a trust relationship, ask yourself the following questions:

- How well will (or do) you demonstrate trustworthy behaviors?
- How well will (or does) the other person demonstrate trustworthy behaviors in this situation?
- What is the state of the relationship? Is it new, developing, or long sustained? Is it healthy or dysfunctional?
- Do you implicitly trust the person? With what things do you trust the person? With what things do you not trust the person?
- What do you like about the person and what can you rely on from that person?
- Is there any behavior that has to be confronted? If so, how are you going to handle it?
- What impact will trusting or not trusting a person have on the project or venture?
- What things can you do to build trust fast and strong?
- Are you focusing on costs or value creation? Conversations about value creation enable trust.
- What remedies do you have if things go wrong?

There are also different scenarios, e.g., new versus long-standing relationships, for applying trust in projects or ventures. Here are a few practical tips for projects around trust:

- Differentiate between projects that require working with people who need to earn your trust (on critical components) and those working with people who have already earned your trust.
- For projects/ventures working with people earning your trust, establish a manageable scope for six months to one year so that you can explore opportunities and relationships.
- Place critical components of a trust value chain, or a project, only in hands of people you implicitly trust.
- Develop a trust value chain from a core group of three to 12 people (a group that will hold each other accountable).
- Each group member, identify three people in business or professions they implicitly trust that fit the project/venture.
- Scope project/venture based on capacity within trust boundaries (for critical components).

You also need to assess the health of each key individual trust relationship periodically. In doing so, you need to decide if it needs maintaining, pruning, or cutting and take appropriate action.

Considerations for Value Network Versus Trust Network

Focusing on individual trust relationships helps you discover the quality of the relationships within your network, which will help leverage available assets and resources. However, it's important to understand exactly what exchanges, flows, and deliverables occur within your network so you know what you can leverage.

While not covered here, it is easy enough to frame your network in terms of value by asking the following questions:

- Who are the people (or roles) in the network?
- What deliverables, exchanges, and flows occur in the network?
- Who is involved with each deliverable, exchange, and flow in the network?

- How well do the deliverables, exchanges, and flows occur with the people involved?
- From the previous elements, what value lies in the network?
- How can you improve and leverage the value in the network?

The best of all worlds is where you have a network filled with high-trust and high-value. Choices of whom to work with should be a combination of trust and the value each person brings. However, this is not a typical scenario unless you have been working on it with intent.

If you have a situation where someone brings high-value, but adequate trust is not present, see if you can discover a scope that allows for adequate trust and still takes advantage of the high-value the person brings. If you trust the person, but they do not bring sufficient value to the project, see if you can discover a scope that will bring forth the value and take advantage of the trust.

In either situation, if you cannot find an equation that brings both sufficient trust and value, I recommend that you walk away for the time being.

People and the Trust Network

This chapter has focused on how to leverage trust to transform global business opportunities. As with any methodology though, it can become mechanistic when focus is placed on the tasks and activities of managing trust rather than the people involved.

What was presented here should be used as a guideline and framework for facilitating trust relationships so you can see improved business performance. However, if you lose your connection to the people in the process, you defeat your initial purpose and the power of the trust network.

To keep yourself grounded, ask yourself the following questions:

- Do I care about the relationships and people within the network?
- Am I serving and looking out for the interests of the people in the network, even if it means sacrifices on my part?
- Is what I'm doing helping or harming people?
- What will I lose if I lose the trust of these people?
- Is what I am doing worth losing the trust?

Remember, the common denominator in any organization, community, society, market, or industry is the people involved. People are the reason that these spheres exist and people are the reason we are able to create wealth. If we harm or abuse them, it can directly impact profitability.

Conclusion

Most consider trust an intangible asset, if an asset at all. But while it may not take physical form as currency, it is tangible in the behaviors exhibited by people in relationships.

High-trust relationships provide many benefits for businesses, including faster execution, lower costs, and even improved competitive advantage. These relationships situated in networks of business interests direct where flows of capital, information, resources, and assets go.

Trust networks employ the methodology of using trust, along with value, to configure business strategy for global business. Trust networks are developed in steps – from trust relationships, to trust value chains, to trust networks.

Individuals are the lowest common denominator in trust networks, so how individuals trust themselves and others and how well those relationships develop mutual trust, impact the health of the entire network.

Using a trust network to strategically leverage business opportunities is the macro level, but the trust network itself must be facilitated first and primarily through the micro level which are the relationships themselves.

9

Designing, Planning, and Implementing Going Global Projects

Up to this point, the book has been focusing on the first four steps of the Going Global on a Dime (GGD) process: 1) Identifying opportunities, 2) Gaining knowledge about business environments and issues, 3) Identifying and leveraging strengths you have or that others have, and 4) Building an ecosystem to support your business model. From a timeframe perspective, you focus on these first four steps for three to six months before you start narrowing down your opportunities, although you will continue to do the steps as a part of the going global process.

You will likely feel overwhelmed with the amount of information and possible opportunities if you have worked the process correctly. You should have more options than you originally thought as there are numerous opportunities in emerging and frontier markets. You should have identified several different pathways to execute these opportunities as well.

All the opportunities you hold on to for consideration for immediate, or near term, execution should be rooted in the strengths you have available to you – your strengths and those of others who will commit them to you. If not, you will be waiting for something to happen.

If you haven't already, develop a simple list of the strengths available to you at any time. This list will actually help you sift through opportunities quickly. There will be opportunities you are interested in, but cannot execute because you do not have the appropriate strengths. You can still hold onto these for the future. You want to choose opportunities in which you are interested, that fit into your long-term objectives, and for which you have the strength to execute at some level immediately or in the near term.

Once you have worked through the first four steps of the GGD process iteratively and come up with a decent list of potential opportunities, you now want to shift to passing through the funneling process to identify one, or a few, key opportunities to pursue.

Prioritizing Opportunities and Choosing Key Projects

Prioritizing opportunities and choosing key projects is the fifth step of the GGD process as mentioned in the chapter entitled *The Going Global on a Dime Process*. The first activity is to complete a brief SWOT analysis on each of the opportunities you are considering. Doing so will make it easier for you to compare them as you prioritize and finally choose between them.

Draw a matrix like the one below and place key points for each of the categories – Strengths, Weaknesses, Outcomes, and Threats.

Strengths	**Outcomes**
Weaknesses	**Threats**

I have changed "opportunities," in this case, to "outcomes" so there is no confusion between the business opportunity you are considering and the outcomes you anticipate. For example, establishing a beachhead in Nigeria for food products after taking up the opportunity to establish a local dairy farm in a region with no dairy farms is an example of a positive, anticipated outcome.

Strengths and weaknesses take a look at your internal issues in executing the opportunity. Outcomes and threats look at the external context of executing the opportunity.

When you are looking at each SWOT analysis, also note how you could eliminate, mitigate, or overcome the weaknesses and threats. This will all be part of your consideration for which business opportunities you will pursue.

Next, you need to set criteria for choosing business opportunities to pursue. Any opportunity chosen must fit within the frame of a small, but significant project. The goal is to be able to use the strengths available to you to create a beachhead, or a platform, which will open other doors for you or grow into a large opportunity itself. You are looking for something that, when you invest any effort into it at all, it should allow you to create a huge impact. Think of something that you will be able to scale quickly, might be able to create other products off of quickly, might be able to reach different audiences quickly, etc.

You can customize the criteria for choosing the best opportunities; however, the following list represents the baseline criteria you need to use to make use of the GGD methodology most effectively:

- Provides value to clients and stakeholders.
- Can implement using existing resources & capital.
- Can deliver with excellence and quality with available capacity.
- Can implement within 3 to 6 months.
- Is easy to implement.
- Takes business to the next level.
- Generates cash flow within one year.

Now, develop a business opportunity prioritization matrix, which allows you to rank each project side by side. You can easily generate one on paper, or in a word processor or spreadsheet program. The following image is a sample.

Opportunity	Criteria 1 Value	Criteria 2 Delivery Excellence	Criteria 3 Start in 3-6 months
Opportunity 1	2	5	3
Opportunity 2	**5**	**5**	**1**
Opportunity 3	4	2	2
Opportunity 4	1	5	1

Use a scale of 1 to 5 (low to high) to rate each opportunity on each criteria. After doing so, total the scores for each opportunity.

Your top three opportunities will generally be the ones you decide to pursue for the time being. However, you should take a fresh look at your SWOT analyses, background information, criteria, and rankings to make sure you agree with them before moving forward on the top choices.

Designing, Planning, and Implementing the Opportunity

After you have chosen opportunities to pursue, you need to develop an implementation strategy which includes a business model, concept document, action plan, and budget. In the chapter entitled *Leveraging to Take Advantage of Opportunities,* I mentioned key elements of the business model.

You can learn more about how to develop a business model and concept document from a short webinar[40] I have prepared. In addition, you can subscribe to a weekly email newsletter[41] that shares tools and further techniques to use with the GGD process for the first year of preparation and execution.

---

[40] http://www.afribiz.info/content/the-business-model-the-heart-of-the-business-plan
[41] Go to www.globalbizconcierge.com and subscribe to the "Going Global Basic Tools" list.

Sample Project: Single Country, Single Product Model

Single Country, Single Product (SCSP) is one sample of a small, but significant project framework we use. In essence, we find a single product that we believe will have high demand in key urban areas in a particular country, then work to place that product in one of the larger urban centers. This is a good model to help you establish a beachhead, or small footprint, in a country.

You are using the single product to build a platform so you can bring in other products and services into markets in the country and region. By focusing on one product that will have high demand, you should be able to generate cash flow sooner while keeping costs reasonable. You have to partner with a local company to execute this because you will rely on their knowledge of the markets and business environment.

Costs remain reasonable because instead of dealing with costs to introduce several products at one time you are only focusing on one. For example, if you want to introduce several products in one of the major store chains in South Africa, you need to pay them approximately $2,500 per product and you typically have to fund the initial inventory in this model.

Also, you use existing infrastructure as much as possible, e.g., your local partner's business infrastructure, to operate in the country instead of establishing your own company at first. This also helps to reduce costs. You work together through a joint venture agreement and then you can look to convert that to a legal entity when it seems reasonable.

Sample Implementation Process

With the SCSP model, we have developed a standard implementation process with standard documentation. It's designed to be both simple and easy to manage as you do not want to get bogged down in project management details.

First, you need to make sure you have the proper documentation in place with partners, and or investors. Make sure you have executed non-compete/non-disclosure agreements and letters of intent, or memorandum of understanding. Letters of intent will indicate what venture you are working on together, key resources committed by stakeholders, responsibilities of each stakeholder, and general processes for handling expenses, revenue, and profit. The letter of intent is just to establish the general working framework while the detailed project documents like project scope, plan, and budget provide what will be necessary to execute on a day-to-day basis.

A good place to get common documents used in international trade is the International Chamber of Commerce (ICC).[42] The ICC focuses on organizations that work across borders, so their model documents and templates are designed to accommodate international business and trade.

The key role that has to hold everything together is the project lead, which in many cases, will be you. However, this person should have basic project management skills. This makes a significant difference in the ability to execute. You can easily find resources about project management online. I have a basic project management workshop[43] that I put together which you can download for free.

Other roles include the local partner who will execute the going global project in the country. You may have an implementation facilitator that works between you and the local partner on the ground. For instance, you are working closely with an individual from that country who connects businesses in your home country and those in the foreign country. The implementation facilitator helps smooth the bumps in the road for all parties who are geographically and culturally dispersed. Typically, the implementation facilitator is a partner as well.

Another typical role is equity partner, or investor. These are people who choose just to invest funds for the project, or venture. However, before you can generally approach individuals like this, you have to have the project ready to go. Most investors need a clear understanding of what the venture is, how the money is going to be used, and how they will get back their investment with returns.

---

[42] http://www.iccwbo.org
[43] http://www.lauri-elliott.com/wp-content/uploads/pmbasics.pdf

Travel to the country of operation should be incorporated into the plan. The first trip should be during the designing phase. It will give you direct input as to the business environment, local partner, market, etc. in which the product will be deployed. If possible, the project lead and implementation facilitator should take the trip together. The second trip should be just after the project is kicked off and the operations have begun on the ground. And a third trip should be done 9-12 months after to see how well things have progressed and to get ready to transition to the next phase. These trips will typically be one to two weeks in length each.

You can virtually eliminate travel if you have a strong local partner who you trust as I spoke of in the chapter entitled *Leveraging Trust Networks*. However, this usually comes from knowing someone, as well as his or her competencies, work habits, etc. over a period of time. It may not be difficult finding such a person as many people who have left their home countries to study or work in developed nations are returning home or establishing themselves between the two countries for business or professional concerns. In fact, people in this role are one of the most powerful partners you can have.

The first year of your project starts when you have your kickoff meeting, not when you are taking care of all of the preliminary work. The preliminary work needs to be finalized before the kickoff meeting. For example, if you need basic documents, funds transferred, and resources to get started, make sure you have them before your kick-off meeting. Sometimes these preliminary details can take upwards of a year, so take your time and be thorough because once you have your kickoff meeting you don't want to have to worry about any of those details anymore. Ask yourself, if you have the kickoff meeting today, will you be ready to implement your plan tomorrow? If not, there is still work to be done.

Regular reporting should occur. It should cover your key tasks and accomplishments, open tasks, what comes up next, key issues, and financials. You want to be transparent with your stakeholders and equity contributors.

Your status report should progress according to objectives and project plan. If not, it should indicate why and how the situation will be corrected.

As a part of writing up your status reports, you are going to need to get together with your local partner and find out how things are going on his end. You might find that local partners are good at executing but not in reporting. Since this information is valuable and needed, it is advised that you either sit down with them, Skype or have a phone call and ask them about what progress is being made. You can be flexible with this, do it over coffee or dinner if you'd like.

It is important not to sound like you are trying to micromanage them, they should be happy to discuss this with you. Ask your partner the questions that you need answers to and record or write down what is said. This will help to fill out your report to the stakeholders with information that you are not dealing with on a daily basis and it will also let you know how things are going.

For partners that are working on the project regularly and directly, you will find that you will meet informally as needed. However, you should always have a formal meeting for the key project executors at least once a month. You always want to try and keep your status meetings to one hour or less. If issues come up, and you need to talk longer, then ask if you can extend the meeting or schedule another one. You don't want to have these meetings drag on, especially if there is a big time difference, so always schedule them for only an hour.

If you have equity contributors that are not actively involved in the project, you will want to schedule meetings with them on a quarterly basis. However, they should be receiving the monthly status reports as well.

After your kickoff meeting has been completed and everybody knows what their duties are, your next activity is mobilizing the local partner. The first month will be spent making sure that everything is ready to go in the country where you will be operating. All of the supplies should be there and ready to use. In about 30 days, you should be ready to get your product into the market.

Another goal is to be able to show some revenue generation in the first year. This is why it is so important to have a lot of the busy work and planning taken care of with your preliminary work before the kickoff meeting. You do not want to have things slowdown in the foreign country.

It's also important to keep a rhythm. There will likely be delays, but do not let the project just sit. Always look for workarounds to keep it going.

Months 2 and 3 are your country start months. This is where you roll your product out into the market and do market research. First you want to do a brief survey of the market and sales channels. You want to know that your partners are thinking about how they are going to implement your product into the market. You are also going to need to be concerned with validating how your product will be imported and distributed going into the future.

Typically, your first shipment will be small. You want to see how the process is going to work and understand it. You also want to make sure you know your distribution and sales channels.

Other key tasks you need to take care of are obtaining any local permits, etc. that you need to operate or sell and having your local partner set up a bank account specifically dedicated to this going global venture and/or your activities together. If at all possible, you should have online viewing capabilities to the account so you can see how money is flowing in and out of the account.

When you initially roll out your product for the market test, you do not have to worry about getting a large quantity of your product into the country right away. Start with a quantity that will be easy for you to manage and store, you are just trying to see how the public responds to your product at first so that you can make changes, where they need to be made, for full operation of the project. With the initial introduction you are trying to learn a little more about your consumer, how they are going to react to your product and what challenges you will have to overcome to give your product a mass appeal.

Your goal from day 1 is to make money, so you have to have a model that is centered on low cost to enter the market but will also generate cash flow. It is of utmost importance that you make sure for every item you sell, you design the pricing structure to make profit unless you have the financial bandwidth to handle ongoing costs. You will have to give out samples, but your goal is to be making money off of every item that you sell.

While you want to make profit on every sale, you need to figure out the price at which a good number of people in the market are willing to pay. Affordability, if you remember, is a key issue in emerging consumer markets.

Now that you have done some market research with your product you can spend months 4-5 marketing and selling your product to the open market. You will be taking all of the things that you have learned; from your baseline work, in terms of marketing ideas, sales channels and distribution channels, and you are now truly implementing them. It may start out on a small scale, but you should be good to go and at a point where you can start marketing and selling to the local market.

This is when you start making sure that all of your business processes are working smoothly and in harmony. As the project lead, you will be making sure that the supply gets to the local partner, everything is being properly reported, and key responsibilities are being executed. You are going to have to step up now and make sure that things are running correctly and efficiently.

People can tend to make this more difficult than it has to be, but keeping things simple will make people more willing to work with you. If you can manage your project correctly, you will be able to avoid a lot of common mistakes associated with new projects.

Also, as the project lead, you need to have structure but you need to be flexible enough to adapt if something is not working for you. This doesn't have to be a burdensome task, if you have the proper structures in place and strong partnerships you will have every opportunity to be successful.

After the initial six months or so, everything begins to repeat. Do a half-year business venture brief, which means that you bring everyone up to date, similar to your quarterly meeting but slightly bigger. This brief should be designed to celebrate what you all have accomplished so far.

In your last quarter, before your decide if you are going to exit or create a formal business, start to think about the transition you will make. Go over your documents and numbers and decide where you want to go from there. As you have been holding quarterly meetings and sending out monthly status reports, you should have plenty of documentation to help you and the stakeholders make an informed decision. You ideally want to start thinking about all of this in month 10, so that you have time to discuss it with your partners before the first year comes to a close.

At the end of your venture transition (the end of the first year), you will bring everyone together and distribute the profits or reinvest in the venture, which is highly advisable. If you didn't make a profit, the stakeholders will need to consider if they want to continue incurring the financial and resource burden, how things might need to change, etc. And finally, the stakeholders need to decide whether to move forward with the venture or not.

Up to this point, implementation reflects the first stage of the SCSP model. However, we are very keen to provide value to the local economy, so establishing additional capacity in the host country that will spread the economic opportunity through jobs or local entrepreneurs is part of our initial design. It is important to look at bringing this component in as soon as possible, but no later than year 3.

The following outline provides a list of key activities in chronological order with a focus on common elements done to manage a new going global venture project as discussed in this section. You can easily adapt this for your own use.

1. **Preliminary Work**
    1.1. Sign non-compete, non-circumvention agreement.
    1.2. Provide project plan, product details and memorandum of agreement to prospective equity contributors.
    1.3. Review project plan, product details, and memorandum of agreement.
    1.4. Sign memorandum of agreement and transfer equity funds.
    1.5. Send official notification to stakeholders of project start once all memorandums of agreement and transfers of equity funds have been received.

2. **Project Start (Month 1)**
   2.1. Conduct half-hour project kick-off meeting online (phone and/or internet).
   2.2. Complete pre-work for implementation workshop with local partner in target country.
   2.3. Purchase samples and initial consignment of product to introduce to channels in target country.
   2.4. Schedule and make arrangements for implementation workshop in target country.
   2.5. Complete and distribute monthly status report to stakeholders.

3. **In-Country Start (Months 2-3)**
   3.1. Conduct in-country implementation workshop with local partner.
   3.2. Complete brief survey of market and sales channels.
   3.3. Validate import and distribution process for product.
   3.4. Submit for any local permits necessary.
   3.5. Set-up in-country bank account.
   3.6. Complete brief market test.
   3.7. Complete and distribute monthly status reports to stakeholders for months 2 & 3.
   3.8. Conduct one-hour quarterly status meeting with equity contributors online.

4. **Marketing and Sales Process Start (Months 4-5)**
   4.1. Document a brief marketing and sales plan based on inputs from previous work.
   4.2. Approve brief marketing and sales plan.
   4.3. Finalize administrative processes for project.
   4.4. Start regular product sales according to marketing and sales plan.
   4.5. Conduct monthly status meetings with local partner online.
   4.6. Report monthly outcomes and issues to project administrator.
   4.7. Complete and distribute monthly status reports to stakeholders for months 4 & 5.

5. **Half-Year Business Venture Brief (Month 6)**
   5.1. Continue sales and supporting processes.
   5.2. Complete a Half-Year Business Venture Brief, reviewing outcomes and issues to date and recommendations for the final six months of start-up year.
   5.3. Complete and distribute monthly status report to stakeholders for month 6.
   5.4. Conduct one-hour quarterly status meeting with equity contributors.

6. **Updated Business Venture Model Implementation (Months 7, 8, 9)**
   6.1. Continue sales and supporting processes in alignment with updated business venture model recommended in Half-Year Business Brief.
   6.2. Complete and distribute monthly status reports to stakeholders for months 7, 8 & 9.
   6.3. Conduct one-hour quarterly status meeting with equity contributors.

7. **Business Venture Transition (Months 10, 11, 12)**
   7.1. Continue sales and supporting processes.
   7.2. Prepare and distribute documentation outlining long-term arrangements and business process two months prior to year end to stakeholders.
   7.3. Complete and distribute monthly status reports to stakeholders for months 10, 11 &12.
   7.4. Conduct one-hour quarterly status meeting with equity contributors.
   7.5. Distribute first profit to venture partners.
   7.6. Sign long-term joint venture agreement.

Conclusion

So there you have it, the Going Global on a Dime process in all of its glory. This process will take you from investigating opportunities to executing an initial, or first stage, project.

Remember, it is designed to help you take advantage of opportunities in a way that mitigates risk and improves your ability to navigate business opportunities. It assumes that while you will get educated on going global issues, research, prepare, and plan that you will also learn as you go. It is designed to give you enough structure to be flexible, but provide checks and balances to make sure you stay on course.

10

Conclusion and Key Points

Starting your own business is perhaps one of the most exciting adventures on which you can embark. It's the excitement of being able to be your own boss, having the opportunity to share your ideas and inventions with the world, being the person making all of the big decisions, and leading a team that you put together yourself.

Going Global on a Dime was written to help people just like you, entrepreneurs and small business owners, make the transition to global marketplaces. After reading this book, I am sure you have taken note that there are a lot of challenges to overcome in global business. Many of these challenges we simply do not face in our day-to-day lives here in the developed world, such as poor infrastructure and informal business practices. However, these are challenges that can be overcome. And keep in mind that one of the biggest advantages of going global to access developing markets is that they are experiencing a period of growth right now that will probably never be seen in the developed world again.

Going global is a learning process for everyone who does it and in the long run the benefits will far outweigh the negatives. Following the high-level framework presented in this book will help keep you on track but also keep flexibility for new opportunities and issues that arise.

There are two things that I cannot stress enough about going global – do sufficient research and form key partnerships. Nearly every chapter stresses these points because they will prove to be invaluable.

While this book is designed to help people take their businesses global, there will be people who read it and decide that this route is not for them. That's okay. But there are plenty of tips, ideas, and strategies that can help you build your business domestically until one day you feel that you are ready to take it global. There are a lot of great examples of this in chapter two when the topic of key perspectives is discussed. For example, no matter where you are in the world if you want to have a successful and unique business then you are going to need to identify your unique competitive space.

And finally, no matter where you position your business just remember that you are still part of the fabric of the global economy.

Key Points

This section presents key points that were covered in each chapter.

Chapter 1 - Introduction

- Multinationals are already thriving in the global economy and so can you. Developing markets are growing at a much faster rate than the markets in developed nations and they need just about everything, but it takes the right person to be able to deliver it to them.

- There are challenges to entering these markets that you would not necessarily face domestically including market entry challenges, environmental challenges and business culture, customs and protocol challenges.

- Challenges can be overcome by using various tactics and tools, which include doing thorough research and due diligence; seeking assistance through government agencies (especially in U.S.); obtaining necessary business licenses and getting familiar with the regulatory standards; learning about their culture and language; dealing with one, or a few, opportunities at a time; and forming strong partnerships and winning favor in the local community.

- Explore different market entry portals to find the best way to take your business abroad. Some market entry portals include partnering with another company, franchising opportunities, commercial subcontracting, and two-way trade partnerships.

- Pay attention to your triple bottom line – people, planet, and profit. The goal here is to not simply harvest resources from a country and then leave it. Add value.

Chapter 2 – The Going Global on a Dime Process

- The three main categories that international business is divided into are income, investment, and trade.
- Keep in mind the key perspectives that will be important to you and the success of your business. Finding your unique competitive space and creating value are two items that you should mold your business around.
- There are a variety of key entrepreneurial tactics that you can utilize to give yourself the best chance of having success in a global setting. Some of these tactics include serving and seeding others; using what you have; seeking knowledge; collaborating with others; and working on a shoestring budget and staying out of debt. The GGD process has an 18-month horizon on average and there are four steps you will do simultaneously and iteratively - identifying opportunities, gathering knowledge about the business environment in which you will be working, recognizing and leveraging your strengths to take advantage of business opportunities, and developing the ecosystem that will support the success of your global venture from suppliers to distributors to partners to consumers.
- The remaining steps in the GGD process include prioritizing opportunities and choosing key projects, generating business model and concept document, develop implementation plan, and implement and evaluate.

Chapter 3 – Opportunities and the Business Environment

- The Going Global on a Dime (GGD) process focuses on doing business in a foreign country more than trade or investment. It is not about going global and spending no money, but about how to leverage the cash, and other resources, you have to go global.
- In preparation for the GGD process you need to assess where you are in terms of readiness.

- A simple framework for identifying opportunities is MADE – market, assembly (or manufacturing), distribution (or agent), and existing business.
- The best market opportunities are those that start with fulfilling a need.
- Identify a project that will give you sufficient rewards with a level of risk that you are willing to take on.
- Build country and opportunity profiles, using frameworks provided in Appendix B and C.
- For every issue you face in a domestic market, you have the same in other markets and more. Doing adequate research will help you navigate this complex facet of going global.

Chapter 4 – Managing Intellectual Property

- Intellectual property (IP) is a collection of legal rights that protect the creative work of individuals, although the intellectual property can obviously become owned by corporations.
- Forms of IP include trademarks, copyrights, patents, industrial design, and trade secrets.
- Partner selection is the most important step when deciding to share your IP. Focus on developing relationships with your business partners, contracts alone are not the best forms of protection for IP.
- Partner with someone for a smaller project before going into large joint venture or strategic alliance together.
- Define how your idea can be compromised by others and who those culprits would most likely be and decide if there are any legal steps that you need to take to prevent this from happening, like obtaining a trademark or patent.

Chapter 5 - Due Diligence

- Due diligence is essentially when you try to get to know as much about a specific business, business market, or partner as you can. It is a method to minimize risk and increase likelihood of expected outcomes. If you are going to make a decision with a significant amount of money at stake you want your decision to be as informed as possible.

- Transaction due diligence is done in preparation for a business deal. As a buyer, you want to be assured that you will get the product you asked for. As the seller, you want to be assured you get paid and that the good or service you are providing will be used in way that is a positive reflection of your company.

- Partnership due diligence is necessary because business success is tied to relationship success with consumers, suppliers, partners, etc. Strong healthy relationships help you leverage better and bigger opportunities.

- The fact that you need to do due diligence, which may include requesting official documentation and facts, is not an issue but how you do it can be. It might be offensive to some businesspeople in developing nations to ask for business information upfront. You can find gracious ways of doing due diligence, instead of framing your conversations with demands for information, focus on learning about and showing interest in your potential partner.

- When larger risks are involved, it is advisable to visit, meet, and observe the potential partner in their natural setting. This affords you the opportunity to collect due diligence information informally and build personal relationships.

- Investment due diligence is simply the process by which a potential investor evaluates and becomes better acquainted with a potential investment in order to get a better understanding of the risks and rewards that the investment offers. When conducted correctly, due diligence offers potential investors the opportunity to act with higher levels of confidence and can be the difference between profitability and loss.

- There are three different types of due diligence used to assess risk in investment; legal due diligence, financial due diligence and market due diligence.
- Secondary sources, like chambers of commerce, can provide a lot of valuable information about a company you are thinking about doing business with. You will also need to check some primary sources though like a customer, partner, employee, or someone who deals with the company you are interested in on a regular basis.

Chapter 6 – Leveraging to Take Advantage of Opportunities

- The Leverage Point Strategy™ is a specific methodology based on the concept of leverage. The goal is to see a small force produce as much change in output as possible.
- Leverage points are simply tangible and intangible assets, resources, situations, etc. that can be used to gain and sustain momentum in the business environment. Almost anything can be considered a leverage point, but you focus on identifying those in your favor with high impact potential.
- The Law of the Few, the Stickiness Factor, and the Power of Context are examples of leverage points, which can cause tipping points as described in *Tipping Points: How Little Things Can Make a Difference*.
- There are a wide range of capital types, which can be used as leverage points. They include economic, social, spiritual, knowledge, political, environmental, creative, positional, institutional, physical, generational, closeness and relational.
- Common leverage points to review in the global business environment are consumer demographics, trade and investment agreements, economic zones and clusters, cities and economic hubs, language and culture, and demand-driven opportunities.

Chapter 7 – Powering Your Own Going Global Network

- Being a global organization is not just a mantra for tapping marketplaces around the world. It is, in fact, a new paradigm shift – a new reality. Today, even small firms are being born global and finding success.

- Going global is not a matter of what you have, but also into what you can tap. In this connected world, you are only a few steps away from people who can help you find the right people, right resources, right information, and right capital.

- At the heart of every successful firm today, is a network, or ecosystem, which is both internal and external to the organization. Your goal is to become the network facilitator of an ecosystem that will support your business venture. You will not own the majority of resources and assets needed for your business venture, but you will be able to marshal what's needed through your ecosystem.

- To "go global on a dime," means that every resource, asset, knowledge, and bit of cash you put in it goes further because you work with others that bring what they can to the table, allowing all of you to go further. You need to be able to identify the value held within your networks and leverage it to shape your business strategies.

- Network weavers look like people we call "social butterflies," but they network, or cross-pollinate ideas, resources, and opportunities for people with a purpose. They also watch, weave, and wake up networks in order to create value for people.

- Healthy networks should multiply over time and when they do, your access to resources, information, capital, influence, etc. grows.

- While it does take an investment of your time and energy, once your value network is sufficiently established, it will help you tap opportunities faster and with less cost and risk overall.

- The process of network weaving promotes the creation of goodwill, a social currency. When someone has goodwill toward you, he or she will more likely share his or her knowledge, assets, and connections with you.

Chapter 8 – Leveraging Trust Networks

- One common denominator in all forms of value exchange is trust. Both sides of the exchange trust they are getting the value expected from the exchange, trusting each other to provide the value expected or agreed upon.

- Trust improves negotiations, increases flow of information, increases ability to learn, increases flexibility in management, increases speed of business transactions, and reduces costs, such as costs of transaction, governing relationships, agency, and opportunity.

- Trust is a strategic asset that you can use to separate yourself from competitors.

- A trust network is an overlay for a value network. The degree and type of trust that exists between people is one factor in determining what value they are willing to exchange and how they view and work in the relationship.

- In the *Speed of Trust*, Stephen Covey identifies characteristics of high-trust leaders, which include being loyal and promoting transparency. There are five waves of trust – self, interpersonal, organizational, market, and society.

- Power trust networks evolve from trust relationships and trust value chains.

- Strategies for going global should build on high-trust, high-value relationships.

Chapter 9 - Designing, Planning, and Implementing a Going Global Project

- All the opportunities you hold on to for consideration for immediate, or near term, execution should be rooted in the strengths you have available to you – your strengths and those of others who will commit them to you.
- Use a SWOT analyses and a business opportunity prioritization matrix to help organize and illuminate opportunities, so you can decide which ones to pursue.
- In the GGD framework, the projects you choose are small, but significant opportunities – those that allow you to create huge impact while using the generally limited resources of an SME or entrepreneur.
- Basic criteria to help you choose opportunities to pursue include capacity to delivery with excellence, can be implemented immediately or in the near term, and provide high value for customers and stakeholders.
- After you have chosen a few opportunities to pursue, you need to develop an implementation strategy which includes a business model, concept document, action plan, and budget.
- One model for going global is the Single Country, Single Product (SCSP). In essence, we find a single product that we believe will have high demand in key urban areas in a particular country, then work to place that product in one of the larger urban centers. This is a good model to help you establish a beachhead, or small footprint, in a country.

Appendix A:
Resources

The following is a list of (mostly free) resources on going global that you may find useful:

- Afribiz webinar on how to develop a business model and concept document - http://www.afribiz.info/content/the-business-model-the-heart-of-the-business-plan
- African Development Bank Group - http://www.afdb.org
- American Chambers Abroad – http://www.uschamber.com/international/directory/default
- A Basic Guide to Exporting 1998 (updated version available for purchase) – http://www.unzco.com/basicguide/
- Bonus Material for Book – bookbonus@conceptualee.com
- Bradley University International Business site - http://www.bradley.edu/academic/colleges/fcba/centers/turner/established/business/
- City Populations – http://www.citypopulation.de
- Culture Grams - http://www.culturegrams.com
- Currency calculator from CNN - http://money.cnn.com/data/currencies/?iid=H_MKT_QL
- Embassy World – http://www.embassyworld.com
- Freelance/Outsourcing Platforms – http://www.guru.com; http://www.freelancer.com; http://www.elance.com; http://www.odesk.com
- Global Edge - http://globaledge.msu.edu/
- Global Export-Import Directory - http://globalexport.usaexportimport.com/
- Global Impact Investing Network - http://www.thegiin.org/cgi-bin/iowa/home/index.html
- Going Global Basic Tools weekly newsletter - www.globalbizconcierge.com

- Government websites around the world - http://www.politicsresources.net/official.htm
- International Chamber of Commerce (ICC) – http://www.iccwbo.org
- International Franchise Association - http://www.franchise.org/
- International Monetary Fund (IMF) –_http://www.imf.org
- International Trade and Tariff Data – http://www.wto.org/english/res_e/statis_e/statis_e.htm
- Millennium Challenge Corporation - http://www.mcc.gov/
- National Cultural Orientation Comparisons – http://www.geert-hofstede.com/hofstede_dimensions.php
- National District Export Council U.S. – http://www.districtexportcouncil.com/
- Newspapers around the world - http://www.abyznewslinks.com/
- Open access data at the World Bank – http://data.worldbank.org
- Project management workshop free download - http://www.lauri-elliott.com/wp-content/uploads/pmbasics.pdf
- Resources for doing business and investing in emerging markets – http://www.afribiz.info; http://www.globalbizconcierge.com
- Reuters Global Investing Blog - http://blogs.reuters.com/globalinvesting/
- Small Business and Entrepreneurship Council - http://www.sbecouncil.org/home/
- The World Bank Group - http://www.worldbank.org/
- Trade Finance Guide: A Quick Reference for U.S. Exporters – http://trade.gov/media/publications/abstract/trade_finance_guide2008desc.html
- U.K. Trade and Investment - http://www.ukti.gov.uk/export/countries.html
- U.S. Agency For International Development - http://www.usaid.gov/
- U.S. Census Bureau Foreign Trade - http://www.census.gov/foreign-trade/

- U.S. Chamber of Commerce, International Division – http://www.uschamber.com/international/default.htm
- U.S. EXIM Bank list of companies that will do credit checks - http://www.exim.gov/pub/ins/pdf/eib99-08.pdf
- U.S. Export Portal – http://www.export.gov
- U.S. Export Programs Guide – http://www.trade.gov/publications/pdfs/epg_2009.pdf
- U.S. International Trade Administration - http://trade.gov/
- U.S. International Trade Administration guide for U.S. exporters - http://trade.gov/media/publications/pdf/trade_finance_guide2007.pdf
- U.S. International Trade Commission Trade Database - http://dataweb.usitc.gov/
- U.S. National Export Initiative (NEI) Site – http://www.export.gov/nei/index.asp
- U.S. Small Business Administration - http://www.sba.gov/
- U.S. State Department – http://www.state.gov
- U.S. Trade and Development Agency - http://www.ustda.gov/
- United Nations - http//www.un.org
- United Nations Conference on Trade and Development (UNCTAD) – http://www.unctad.org
- Who Owns Whom Database – https://solutions.dnb.com/wow/
- World Chambers Directory – http://chamberdirectory.worldchambers.com/
- World Factbook – https://www.cia.gov/library/publications/the-world-factbook/index.html
- World Intellectual Property Organization - http://www.wipo.int
- World Integrated Trade System (WITS) – http://wits.worldbank.org
- World Trade Organization trade policy reviews - http://www.wto.org/english/tratop_e/tpr_e/tpr_e.htm

Appendix B:
Questions for Country Profile

These questions will help you develop a background profile for each of the countries in which you are interested. They are provided by compliments of Regent University's Center for Entrepreneurship.[44]

Geographic
These questions will help you think through and collect information on a country's geography:

- What is the location of this country?
- Are the borders with neighbors safe and secure?
- Are its neighbors of any economic significance?
- What can we glean from this country's history (stability, economic prosperity, social cohesion, etc.)?
- How favorable is the country's climate (moderate, cold, hot, mixture)?
- What are the key natural resources in the country?
- Are there opportunities to explore and better utilize some of the natural resources in this country?

Population
These questions will help you think through and collect information on a country's population:

- What is the total population of this country?
- What is the age structure?
- What is the population growth rate (birth and death rates)?
- What is the net migration rate?
- What is the life expectancy at birth (male and female)?
- What are the major and influential ethnic groups in the country?

---

[44] http://www.regententrepreneur.com

131

- What are the major and influential religions in the country?
- What are the major/official languages?
- What is the rate of literacy (male and female)?

Economy in General

These questions will help you think through and collect information on a country's economy:

- What is the country's GDP in terms of purchasing power parity (PPP) and per capita?
- What is the country's labor force (also classify by occupation)?
- What is the rate of unemployment?
- What is the population below the poverty line?
- What is the inflation rate?
- What is the rate of public debt (i.e. internal and external)?
- What are the country's budgetary allocations (i.e. revenue and expenditure)?
- What is the country's industrial production growth rate?
- How much is the country exporting and importing?
- Who are the country's trading (import and export) partners?
- What are the country's major imports, exports and other natural resources?
- Is the country receiving any foreign aid?
- What is the country's exchange rate (local currency) against the major world currencies (U.S. dollar or British pound)?
- What is the country's GDP (official exchange rate), and GDP (real growth rate)?

Government

These questions will help you think through and collect information on a country's government:

- What type of government does the country have?
- Who are the governing authorities in this country?
- What are the various arms of the government?
- What are the administrative divisions?
- When did this country attain independence?
- Is the country politically stable?

Macroeconomic Situation – Monetary Policy

These questions will help you think through and collect information on a country's monetary policy:

- Are there any inflationary tendencies in the country?
- What are the current interest rates?
- What are the current fluctuations/changes in currency exchange rates?
- Who controls the rate of inflation and interest rates?

Macroeconomic Situation – Fiscal Policy

These questions will help you think through and collect information on a country's fiscal policy:

- How much tax do people and businesses pay to the government in order for it to meet its expenditure?
- How much tax do foreign nationals/expatriate staff and foreign businesses pay to the government?
- Does the government have a fiscal deficit currently?
- From whom does the government borrow money from in order to offset its fiscal deficit (issuing bonds, getting foreign aid, etc.)?

Extent of the Rule of Law

These questions will help you think through and collect information on the rule of law within a country:

- What is the state of the country's stability in terms of enforcement of laws and contracts?
- Does the country guarantee individual political rights and civil liberties?
- Does the country allow individual ownership of property and thus guaranteeing private property rights?
- Are intellectual property rights respected and protected in this country?
- Is there freedom of expression and free and independent media?
- Does the state guarantee security of people and assets from theft, kidnapping and terrorism?
- What is the legal climate and what legal protections currently support commercial transactions in this country?

International Trade

These questions will help you think through and collect information on international trade related to a particular country:

- Are international companies permitted to export to this country?
- What is the average and longest time (in days) to clear direct exports through customs?
- What is the average and longest time (in days) to claim imports from customs?
- What is the percentage of firms that export directly from this country?
- What is the average time (in days) firms spend in meetings with tax officials?
- What are the country's custom requirements and import duties?
- What export goods/products are prohibited from this country?
- Are there reports of fraudulent activities about business in this country?

- What is the best way (i.e. cheapest) to send goods/products into this country?
- What are the absolute and comparative advantages in terms of goods/products in this country?
- Does this country have any regional trade agreements on tariffs and trade?
- Is any privatization of state industries and corporations taking place at this time?
- What are the requirements for firms that want to take part in the privatization process?
- What is the procedure/cost of doing business in this country?

Financial and Capital Markets

These questions will help you think through and collect information on a country's financial and capital markets:

- Is financing available for exports to this country?
- What banking services are available in this country (e.g., loans)?
- Who regulates the banking sector?
- How stable are both the stock and bond markets in this country?
- What are the past trends in both the stock and bond markets?
- Is the capital market free from political manipulation?
- What are currency exchanges and inflationary tendencies like in this country?
- Does the corporate world have confidence in the capital market?

Investment in Human Capital

These questions will help you think through and collect information on how a country invests in human capital:

- What kind of healthcare system is in place in this country?
- How much do companies invest in terms of medical insurance for their employees?
- What is the literacy level in this country?
- How much do companies invest in education and training of their employees?
- What is the rate of employment and unemployment in this country?
- What is the wage structure (i.e., highest paid, minimum wage, etc.)?

Development in Industry/Service Sectors

These questions will help you think through and collect information on developments in industry/service sectors in a particular country:

- What are key industry/service sectors in this country?
- What opportunities/niches exist in these industry/service sectors?
- Are there any untapped or growing industry/service sectors?
- How is the competition in these industry/service sectors?
- Are there any undergoing projects/programs (governmental or quasi-governmental) in the country that foreign firms can pursue with assistance from both internal (i.e., banks, government, foundations, etc.) and external funding (i.e., World Bank, IMF, etc.)?

Technological Innovation and Advancement

These questions will help you think through and collect information on technological innovation and advancement in a particular country:

- Does this country invest in Research and Development?
- How much do companies invest in R&D or technology?
- How skilled are the employees in terms of technological know-how?

- How much do companies invest in their employees in terms of being technologically savvy?
- How is technology transferred in this country (e.g., through technical journals or conferences, industrial espionage, licensing or marketing agreements, co-development agreements, training or exchange of personnel, commercial transactions or patents, or through cross-national exchanges among components of multinational enterprises)?
- How is intellectual property (patents, copyrights, trade secrets, know-how, etc.) transferred?

Telecommunications

These questions will help you think through and collect information on telecommunications in a particular country:

- How long (in days) does it take to obtain a telephone connection in this country?
- How long (in days) does it take to obtain an electrical connection into a new facility?
- Are electrical outages and surges common?
- What percentage of the value of sales is likely to be lost due to electrical surges?
- How reliable (speed and consistency) is the internet system?
- What percentage of firms/people uses the web/internet to interact with clients/suppliers?
- Do companies advertise through radio and television in this country?

Physical Infrastructure

These questions will help you think through and collect information on physical infrastructure in a particular country:

- What are the roadways and railways like (i.e. tattered, smooth, safer, etc.)?
- Is the country accessible by water (sea or ocean)?
- Are the airports and harbors safe and secure?
- Are there water supply failures (if so, how often)?
- Which mode of transportation is cheapest and most reliable in various regions of the country?

Foreign Direct Investment (FDI)

These questions will help you think through and collect information on FDI in a particular country:

- What are the business opportunities in this country?
- Can foreign companies currently invest in the country and are they allowed to own property?
- How can companies obtain background information on the nation's companies?
- How difficult/expensive is it for foreign companies to register to do business in this country?
- Who can I contact to find investment opportunities?
- What types of licenses/work permits are required and what is the time frame for them to be obtained?
- What are the requirements for starting a business under this country's law?
- What is the percentage of ownership/shareholding allowed for foreigners?
- Is insurance available for business activity in this country?
- Are this country's banks participating in commercial transactions?
- What is the legal climate and what legal protections currently support commercial transactions in the country?
- Are there any regional bodies/agreements that protect foreign investors in the country?

- What is the procedure for mergers and acquisitions?
- Is there any income or sales tax in place?

Cultural and Social Factors

These questions will help you think through and collect information on cultural and social factors in a particular country:

- How compatible is the social culture with corporate culture in this country?
- Do people/employees have a dichotomy between modern work ethics and their own ethnic/tribal values?
- In general, what are the attitudes of the people/employees toward work, risk and being an entrepreneur?
- What are their attitudes and worldview toward social mobility, and concerning entrepreneurial culture and opportunities for advancement?
- How important are income, wealth and material goods to the people/employees as compared to other aspects of life (such as leisure, time with family and friends, etc.)?

Country's Forecast

These questions will help you think through and collect information on a country's forecast:

- What is this country's economic forecast based on past trends and current conditions?
- What impact will current political, economic, environmental, etc., conditions have on commercial/investment in the country in the near/long term future?

Appendix C:
Questions to Flush Out Going Global Projects

Business Structure

- How do we make application to register company, business license, labor hiring clearances, tax identification number, etc.?
- What business structure should I use – corporate, partnership, joint venture, strategic alliance, hybrid, etc.? What are the strengths and weaknesses of each?
- Do my in-country partner(s) have the appropriate business structure, capacity, and legal standing to carry out the responsibilities of our agreement?

Capacity, Management, and Production

- Where do you find the lowest cost production materials and labor along with quality?
- Where do I find foreign personnel (or partners) to sell my products or manage my facilities?
- How do I train foreign personnel?
- What fringe benefits are legally required for foreign employees?
- If I want to sell in Saudi Arabia, for instance, how do I locate other companies from my country doing business there so I can learn from them?
- What sales representative/distributor arrangements should I make?
- What business support activities do I need, e.g., interpreter, banking, safety and security, transport, housing, business permits, alternative advertising media, exchange controls.
- With international travel so costly, how do I cost effectively supervise my people stationed in a foreign country.
- Will I allow sales representatives to also sell their own or competitor's products?
- What is the availability of security guards and proper fencing?

- What are local sources for materials and supplies?
- What is the availability of skilled and unskilled labor?
- How should we prepare a safety/security checklist for personnel?

Culture

- How should you greet people?
- What do people in the country think about life in general?
- What is appropriate attire?
- How do people in the country respond to foreigners?
- What are motivating forces for people in the culture?
- What are the family and community structures and relationships like in the country? How do they impact the greater society?
- How do people in the culture handle conflict?
- What are appropriate communication styles?
- Under what circumstances in business and social settings, do people relate to each other formally and/or informally?
- What impact do social relationships have on business?
- What is the diet of people in their country? What is their eating style?
- What are particular ways to show respect (or disrespect)?
- How do people enjoy their free time?
- What are the key holidays and traditions?
- What are the attitudes toward health and education?
- How do the generations relate?
- How do women and men function together in the society?
- What values do the people hold dear in general?
- How do people celebrate art and life?
- What gestures are typical in the culture?
- What is business etiquette like?
- What is social etiquette like?
- How do people perceive the world?
- How does a person define his or her identity? Do people value individual or collective identity?
- How do people approach activity?

- What is the pace of life and work?
- How important are goals in planning?
- What are typical goals in life?
- Where does responsibility for decisions lie, e.g., individual, group, elders?
- How do people define and evaluate success?
- How do people solve problems in life and business?
- How do people prefer to learn?
- How do people define or perceive truth?
- How is time valued?
- What type of person is valued and respected?
- How does the culture express itself in art and music?
- What role does religion or faith play in the culture?
- How do people define and perceive integrity?

Communication Channels

- What advertising, promotion, and media options are available?
- What physical communication channels are available – internet, email, phone, TV, radio?
- What are the best methods of communication for each key stakeholder?
- How do I manage communication with key stakeholders overseas?

Markets

- Which markets sport the best demand for your products?
- What are the best ways to sell your products?
- How do I sell to customers who speak a different language?
- Are high customs fees distorting selling prices?
- How can I compete with host country companies when I have to add overseas shipping and customs costs to my prices?
- What specific trade barriers hinder foreign imports or foreign investment, e.g. licensing, exchange control, protected industries?
- Do government regulations restrict the distribution of imported goods? If so, which ones?

- Are statistics available to show economic growth and decline in the country, industries, and consumer markets (GDP, interest rates, inflation rates, annual capital expenditures, imports, exports, wage rates, unemployment rates)? How reliable are the statistics?
- What are the country's demographic trends, age spread, income distribution, geographic dispersion)
- What are directly competing products in the market?
- Who are the main market share competitors, both local and multinational? (Your goal should be to find an open, or new, market.)

Financials and Taxes
- Am I subject to double taxation, once in a foreign country and again in my home country?
- What are the financial reporting requirements and when do financial reports have to be filed?
- Should these reports be verified by an in-country registered audit firm or can it be done by an auditor in my country?
- Will audited consolidated financial statements from your parent company suffice or must the in-country entity be audited separately?
- How do I get an audit done overseas?
- Has a tax information exchange agreement between the home and host country been executed?
- What are the tax rates?
- Is a tax levied on imports or direct sales?
- Is there any tax incentives applied to foreign direct investments?
- Are intra-company transactions across borders taxed?
- Is there a withholding tax on earnings or royalties to be repatriated?

Infrastructure, Logistics and Distribution

- What type of facilities are available – office, production/processing, warehousing, etc.?
- Which means of transport are the most cost effective?
- What are possible distribution channels?
- Do the same import licensing regulations apply to sales representatives, distribution centers, and end users?
- What transport infrastructure exists to connect your facility with markets, suppliers, and ports of entry?
- Are roadways paved? How well are roads, bridges and tunnels maintained?
- Can trucks pass over bridges and through tunnels safely?
- What are the dangers of transport crime?
- What delays or barriers are there at ports of entry and borders?
- Where are economic zones located? What facilities are available within the zones? What are the rental costs?
- What support activities are available in economic zones and what do they cost, e.g., labor recruiting, transport, bookkeeping, and utilities?
- What types of goods and services can be moved through economic zones.
- What type of work can be performed on the goods held in economic zones?
- What restrictions are there on the destination of shipments out the zones (sales to domestic markets, exports to specific countries, worldwide exports, etc.)

Political and Economic Tone between Countries

- What trade and investment agreements exist between my country and the host country, and how can I use them?
- Does more than one political party vie for office? What are the views of each toward continuing economic reform?
- Is the current government favorably or unfavorably disposed to my home country?

- When is the next election? What is the prognosis?
- What is the country's current relationship with my home country's government?
- What other businesses from my home country are operating in the host country?
- What is the official and unofficial attitude on foreign direct investment from my home country in the host country?
- Are major businesses owned or controlled by government?
- Is there a privatization program underway and which businesses are being sold?
- What government regulations restrict the scope of in-country sales personnel?
- What regulations govern contractual relationships with sales representatives?
- Does the government encourage countertrade arrangements?
- What government incentives exist, e.g., reimbursement for labor training costs, exemption from income and other taxes, low interest, long-term financing, exemption from import customs duties, and long-term lease on property?

Lauri Elliott

Lauri Elliott is a strategist with over 25 years of business experience, specializing in global business, innovation, technology, and new ventures and start-ups. As a noted new media broadcaster, author, speaker, and consultant, she helps small and medium-sized enterprises (SMEs) and entrepreneurs bring life and profit to business ideas in tough, turbulent business environments around the globe, with a particular focus on emerging markets, including Africa.

Lauri is the founder of Conceptualee, Inc., under which she created the brands Afribiz™, GlobalBizconcierge™, and The Art of Making Business Happen™.

As the Director of Afribiz™ Media, Lauri has developed a solid reputation as a journalist, broadcaster, and media personality. She is the primary host of Afribiz.fm™, a regular radio show about doing business and investing in Africa.

Lauri sits on the board of advisers for the:

- Blacks in Government (BIG) African Partnership Secretariat
- Center for Global Entrepreneurship and Enterprise Management (CGEEM) at Morgan State University, which focuses on equipping U.S. SMEs to enter international business. In this capacity, she is leading the development of the Emerging Market Information

Team (EMIT), designed to provide information and intelligence particularly useful to SMEs.

- Howard University African Business Club

Recent awards and honors include:

- Honored as a social entrepreneur to watch in Ashoka's ChangemakeHERS campaign for the 100th Anniversary of International Women's Day in 2011.
- For her work on behalf of SMEs, she received recognition from the U.S. Congress for connecting U.S. businesses to business in Africa.

Lauri has authored several books:

- Export to Explode Cash Flow and Profits: Creating New Streams of Business in Asia, Africa, and the Americas with Little Investment
- Creating Wealth by Harnessing Opportunities in Africa: God's Way to Multiply the Assets in Your Storehouses
- Redefining Business in the New Africa: Shifting Strategy to be Successful
- Grow Rich in the New Africa: A Guide to Navigating Opportunities on the Continent

Lauri has contributed chapters to the following academic references:

- Encyclopedia of Social Networking
- E-Governance and Civic Engagement: Factors and Determinants of E-Democracy

Contact Lauri at http://www.lauri-elliott.com.

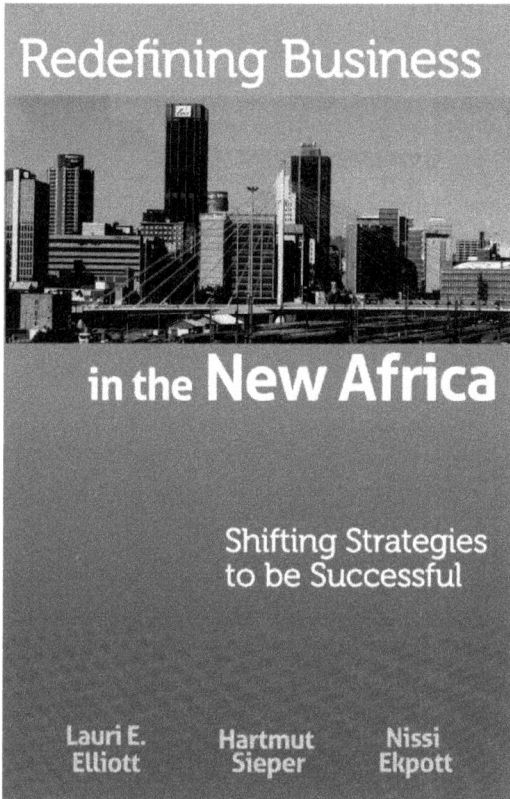

Redefining Business

in the New Africa

Shifting Strategies to be Successful

Lauri E. Elliott   Hartmut Sieper   Nissi Ekpott

www.redefining-business-in-the-new-africa.com

2001-2010 proved to be a transitional decade for Africa, ushering in a new image and status for the continent. Africa began to show it was truly shaking the shackles of its colonial and chaotic past. Now that the New Africa has arrived, what does that mean? And, what does it mean for business?

On almost every issue that has been pegged a negative for Africa – population boom, poverty, disease, governance, economic instability, and conflicts – there is evidence of a growing shift in the other direction. Businesses need to wake up and proactively shift to this new reality, or paradigm. Businesses need to adapt their strategies to the context of Africa to be successful.

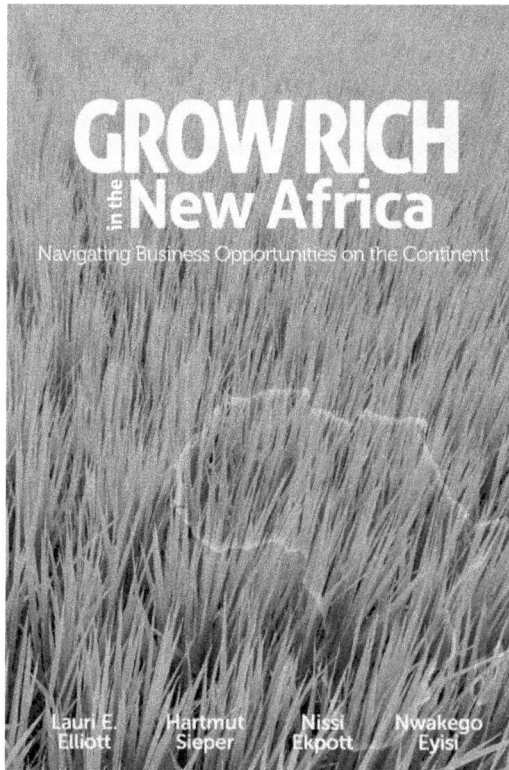

Grow Rich in the New Africa attempts to present a number of opportunities and strategies so that entrepreneurs, investors, and SMEs can piece together unique strategy configurations to be successful in Africa. It extends the coverage first presented in *Redefining Business in the New Africa*. Some of what you will learn includes:

- Global trends and Africa
- Networks of players in Africa
- Business, trade, resource, and information flows in and out of Africa
- The future of major sectors, e.g., energy, real estate, transport, natural resources, retail markets
- Building strategy around both formal and informal markets

Export to
EXPLODE
Cash Flow and Profits

Creating New Streams of Business in
Asia, Africa, and the Americas
with Little Investment

Lauri E. Elliott

www.export-to-explode-cash-flow.com

Exporting is one of the strategies for conducting international business or trade. With the *squeeze* on businesses during the global economic recovery, there is no better time to explore new avenues to generate revenues and profits. *Export to Explode Cash Flow and Profits* specifically shares 12 different leverage points, e.g., demand-driven exporting, multinational ecosystems, and cities and economic hubs that you can use to help formulate strategies for exporting to the emerging markets in Asia, Africa, and the Americas.